NEAR & FAR

NEAR & FAR

Recipes Inspired by Home and Travel

Heidi Swanson

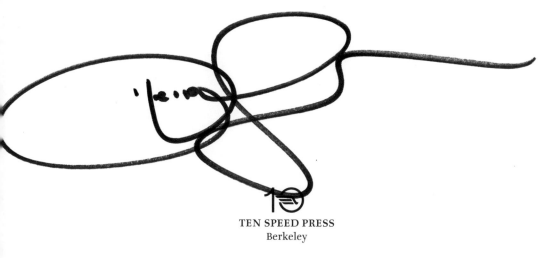

TEN SPEED PRESS
Berkeley

CONTENTS

INTRODUCTION

JANUARY 25—Long, thin whips of deep green puntarelle, a swarm of tiny yellow key limes, dried persimmons with downy skins, red-skinned hand-cracked walnuts, chickpea flour, sprouted mung beans, a friendly giant pomelo with twin glossy leaves attached, stubby bouquets of nameko mushrooms, little yellow pom-poms from snipped branches of acacia tree.

FEBRUARY 15—Fresh fenugreek, ruffled baby cabbage, parrot tulips and buttery freesia blossoms, rose petal jam, French radishes, the tiniest, pointiest green onions, and sprout-fed eggs.

MARCH 22—Helleborus and daffodil, Tahitian pomelo, dried blood oranges, seascape strawberries, amaranth, nettles, fresh pressed olive oil, kumquats, and lazy clusters of fragrant lilacs ranging in hue from pale, dusty purple to electric violet.

Like many cooks, I keep journals. And when you look at mine, you notice cracked spines and paper that is no longer crisp, or clean, or bright. The corners are dull and dog-eared, the pages filled with my handwriting—black ink, the all-caps penmanship I suspect I inherited from my father. Scraps, scrawls, and sketches are taped to lined pages. Newspaper clippings, laser printouts, and magazine snippets commingle in an unruly mob of fonts. There are photos, stamps, receipts, lists, and sticky notes. I keep the journals for a number of reasons, but mostly so I don't forget details—the pattern of an ancient Italian olive grove as seen on approach to the Bari airport, colorful pickles and tiny salads beautifully arranged as part of a bento lunch in Kyoto's Nishiki Market, the markings on the craggy, hand-painted bowls piled high with *fekka* and *chebakia* pastries at a shop in Marrakech, or the impossibly small cherry tomatoes, no larger than blueberries, at Takashimaya in Tokyo. Closer to home, I note the comings and goings of ingredients in my own kitchen, the details of meals shared, and my favorite farmers' market finds week by week.

As I turn the pages of these books, it's clear that much of the food I cook is inspired by two things: where I live (Northern California), and where I've traveled. Food rooted in place—both near and far. This is a cookbook that attempts to explore both.

I'm forty years old now, which means I've lived long enough to settle in a bit. I'm generally happy, curious, and optimistic. I like to think people who know me would concur. My life in San Francisco is a series of rituals and routines. I collect fresh flowers every week. Walk most places I go. Have coffee on Saturday morning with friends. Brew beer with my brother-in-law, but not as often as I'd like. Northern California is where I try to stand still a bit, keep things simple, and watch things change around me. The markets evolve incrementally week after week—poppies giving way to peonies, donut peaches and Pandora leeks giving way to gypsy peppers, amethyst radishes, and purple wax beans. The pruned trees in Golden Gate Park go from twiggy and lifeless to lush, green, and full in a steady march through spring into summer and fall.

Home is good. That said, I started traveling, extensively, as soon as I found a job after college and could afford to. I spent the bulk of my bank account on a flight to Europe, a trip that showed me I could explore far-flung places on my own dollar, sparking a desire to see more of the world I was a part of. In an interview, Pico Iyer said, "It's only by stepping out of your life and the world that you can see what you most deeply care about and find a home. . . . And home, in the end, is of course not just the place where you sleep. It's the place where you stand." Travel inspired my thinking, relationships, sensibility, sense of self, and, eventually, the way I approached cooking. I do my best to explore someplace new, or revisit a place I love, a couple of times a year.

Once you're home from a trip, details tend to fall away. I noticed, long after I've forgotten the names of monuments, train stations, or boulevards of a city I've traveled to, the flavors would stay with me. Every place has its own always evolving culinary voice. And it's not just ingredients and flavors, but also techniques, traditions, and vessels. In the broadest sense, these impressions and memories are what inspire new ideas in my own kitchen as well as spark the urge to re-create dishes or flavor combinations that made the deepest mark.

The Book

The book is divided into two major sections—Near and Far. The Near section focuses on recipes inspired by my life in San Francisco and Northern California. Far is divided into five chapters: Morocco, France, India, Italy, and Japan. These are places with rich, often ancient, culinary cultures—places I've spent a good amount of time, in many cases with extended or multiple trips over a span of years. I've also threaded a few of my favorite travel-friendly preparations into a section titled En Route.

At the start of each chapter, I list favorite ingredients traditionally used in the cuisine of that place (My Moroccan Pantry, My Japanese Pantry, and so on). They are the ingredients that resonate with me and speak to my cooking approach best—they aren't intended to be comprehensive but are more *a sketch* of the ingredients I turn to most or am most enthusiastic about using within that palette. Many are used within the recipes here, but not necessarily all. They're listed this way for quick brainstorming and inspiration in your own kitchen.

Within each chapter, recipes are organized starting with lunch, moving on to dinner, drinks, and treats. I tend to think of the next day's breakfast at the end of the day, so those close out the chapters.

The Recipes

The recipes in this book are rooted in place and correspondingly organized. I tend to be drawn to places where natural foods are celebrated and
traditional foodways are in practice. Much of that influence is woven into
the recipes throughout. That said, it's not the sort of cookbook that is going
to drill down on the nutritional benefits of this pulse or that vegetable—
although those considerations are a part of how I cook and certainly one
aspect of what I think about as I approach a recipe. For those of you who
have *Super Natural Cooking* or *Super Natural Every Day* on your shelf, consider this a companion volume. You'll recognize the spirit of the previous
volumes—real food and powerful vegetarian ingredients made into dishes
that are worth making.

Perhaps some description of my approach will help illuminate how
I came to include the recipes you see here. Everything starts with me
trying to garner a sense of *place,* particularly when I'm traveling. On the
culinary front, I attempt to gain a basic understanding of the traditional
culture of the cuisine I'm immersed in, gather some historical context,
get a handle on what ingredients are typically used and which cooking
techniques are deployed, and understand what people are cooking and
why. A good amount of wandering and meandering is part of my process, punctuated by stops at specific shops, restaurants, stalls, markets,
and establishments I've earmarked ahead of time. Perhaps most impor-
tantly, I seek out my *beat* within other cultures (as well as my own). In
Japan, I tend to focus on many of the macrobiotic and *shojin-ryori* (Zen
Buddhist temple cuisine) preparations and ingredients. Or, related
to India, I like to learn about what ingredients practitioners use for
Ayurvedic treatments, or what they eat daily in an ashram or in a Jain
temple or in the narrow street alleys of Chandni Chowk, Delhi's ancient
market. It's from this vantage point that I begin to think about cooking
and recipe development, and where I often find my own angle, voice,
and technique.

You'll see a mix of recipe types in this book. One recipe was inspired
by Grace Young's passion for cooking with a cast-iron wok, another after
I saw a group of women breaking for lunch on a crowded Delhi sidewalk;
there was a carrot salad I encountered in a snowy mountain monastery
town, and another recipe idea sparked by a favorite Japanese spice blend,
shichimi togarashi. There are recipes inspired by ingredients I've encountered, markets I've shopped, cooks I've chatted up, books I've read, and

scribbles I've made in my journal; there are my takes on regional preparations and others based on snapshots I've taken with my camera.

Stylistically, I have some rules—although *rule* might be too strong a word: *best practices* could be a better term. I tend to work within a regional palette of ingredients. Meaning, you won't see a whole lot of cross-cultural ingredient mixing within recipes or chapters. If I'm cooking with Japanese ingredients, I'll likely use oil from that palette— perhaps sesame. The vinegar might be brown rice vinegar, the noodles buckwheat soba, and the seasoning shoyu or mirin. So I won't often mix, say, shoyu with *ras el hanout* or use preserved lemons with miso. I also tend to do multiple dishes from one region and not serve, for example, a tagine alongside saag paneer.

Many of the recipes lend themselves easily to seasonal adaptations, so keep that in mind—if a recipe calls for asparagus, and it's autumn, consider using broccoli or cauliflower.

Finally, a word about sourcing ingredients. It is understood in many cultures that food is powerful medicine, with whole or natural foods being the most beneficial, interesting, and delicious. Do your best to avoid genetically modified crops or those that have been sprayed intensively with pesticides, or grown in soil that has been fertilized with chemicals known to damage the environment as well as the health of the individuals harvesting your food. Seek out food and ingredients that are healthy, powerful, and full of beauty and vitality—the sort of food that lifts the spirit and sustains the body: food that hasn't been stripped of its natural nutrients and beneficial properties. It matters and it is worth it.

Near

SAN FRANCISCO

SAN FRANCISCO IS MY HOME. I was born an hour south of here at a hospital my mom worked in then, and works in now. I left my parent's home at eighteen but in the end didn't venture far. It's the rolling hills my eyes are used to, and the scent of eucalyptus in the air that lets me know where I am.

San Francisco has always been a beloved yet peculiar city. A nonnative friend aptly described it to me as a place with an "eccentric weft." It is a destination for dreamers and misfits, and for those who like to sit at the edge of the continent and look even farther west. It's where individuals come to make their fortunes, shed conventions, and brave seismic instability. And it's a place of beauty. You can get up high enough at day's end to watch the sun set into the Pacific while its light winks off pastel skyscrapers downtown and west-facing windows lining the Oakland hills. It's against this backdrop that I live and work.

My cooking here is defined by a combination of the weather, the spectrum of produce, the range of textures and flavors and colors dictated by the season at hand. An ever-evolving kaleidoscope of inspiration driven by the people I chat with, the places I eat, the books I pick up, the friends who visit, and the markets I frequent. Our dining room has a long farm table made of dark chestnut, a mob of chairs, and a chandelier that bounces bright prisms off the one mirror in the room. The table is etched with endless scars and scratches, most from before our time with it. But we've certainly made our own marks. We eat most of our meals here—sometimes two of us, sometimes ten, and I think often about how true it is that this table is the heart and focal point of our house.

My San Francisco Pantry

AVOCADOS

CITRUS

CHICORIES

COASTAL SEA VEGETABLES

CULTURED BUTTER

DAIRY

DARK LEAFY GREENS

EDIBLE FLOWERS

FRESH HERBS

HEIRLOOM BEANS

MEYER LEMONS

NUTS AND SEEDS

OLIVE OIL

PASTURED EGGS

RAW HONEY

ROOT VEGETABLES

SALAD GREENS

SPROUTS

STONE FRUITS

WHOLE GRAINS

WINTER SQUASH

Cucumber Salad

lemongrass * tofu * red onion * pine nuts

I'm going to open the book with a recipe I hope will be a tone-setter. It is a substantial salad, the sort I would happily eat any day—though it really hits the spot when the sun is full on. Crisp, snappy cucumbers, earthy pine nuts, kale, and tofu all get tossed with a simple brown sugar–kissed lemon vinaigrette. You can enjoy it on its own, over soba noodles or farro, or atop a mountain of arugula. Look to the picture to get a sense of how thick to slice the cucumbers: you want them quite thin, but not so transparent that they lose all structure. Too thick and they seem a bit crude.

SERVES 4 TO 6

1 large (12 oz | 340 g) cucumber, seeded and thinly sliced

1 small red onion, or 6 spring onions, thinly sliced

1 cup | 1.5 oz | 45 g chopped kale or cilantro

12 oz | 340 g extra-firm tofu, cut into ½-inch | 1.2cm cubes

3 stalks lemongrass, tender center only, minced

¼ cup | 60 ml brown rice vinegar

¼ cup | 60 ml freshly squeezed lemon juice

3 tablespoons natural brown sugar or honey

Scant 1 teaspoon fine-grain sea salt

Scant ½ teaspoon red pepper flakes

½ cup | 3 oz | 90 g toasted pine nuts

1 lime, cut into wedges

Place the cucumber, onion, kale, and tofu in a large mixing bowl.

In a small saucepan over medium heat, combine the lemongrass, vinegar, lemon juice, brown sugar, and salt and simmer for a couple of minutes—long enough for the sugar to dissolve. Remove from the heat and whisk in the red pepper flakes. Let cool for 5 minutes and pour over the cucumber mixture. Toss gently but thoroughly and let sit for at least 15 minutes. Toss again and adjust the salt and red pepper to taste.

To serve, drain off any residual liquid from the cucumber mixture; if you're serving this salad with soba, salad greens, or grains, toss these with this liquid. Top with pine nuts and a good squeeze of lime. Serve the remaining lime wedges at the table.

Fennel Stew

corona beans ✳ saffron ✳ white wine ✳ olive oil

Here a luxurious saffron broth dimpled with olive oil plays host to tender wedges of leeks, onion, and fennel. If you're mindful of the way you slice your ingredients, it becomes a beautiful and elegant bowl of fragrant silky slivers. Part of the reason I call for small fennel and onions is that you can slice them lengthwise into perfect bites. Be sure to wash the fennel and leeks well by immersing them in water and getting in between the layers to dislodge hard-to-see grit. And while tender baby fennel is easiest to work with, any fennel trimmed of tough outer layers then sliced will work well. As far as the beans go, plump corona beans are my first pick, but white cannellini beans are a fine alternative.

SERVES 6

4 small (baby) fennel bulbs, cut into thin wedges, fronds reserved

2 generous pinches saffron (about 40 threads)

Fine-grain sea salt

½ cup | 120 ml extra-virgin olive oil

4 small yellow onions, cut into ¼-inch | 6mm slices through the root end

4 medium leeks, washed, trimmed, and cut into ¼-inch | 6mm slices

6 small cloves garlic, very thinly sliced

2 pounds | 900 g cooked corona beans

⅔ cup | 160 ml dry white wine

2 to 3 cups | 480 to 710 ml warm water (or broth left over from cooking beans)

Feta or goat cheese, chopped oily black olives, and lemon wedges, to serve

Bring a small pot of well-salted water to a simmer and cook the fennel wedges until tender, a couple of minutes. Place in an ice water bath to stop cooking. Drain well and set aside.

Meanwhile, use a mortar and pestle to grind the saffron with ¼ teaspoon of sea salt.

In a large, heavy pot over medium heat, combine the olive oil with the saffron salt and heat until fragrant, just a minute or so. Add the onions and cook, stirring regularly, 10 minutes or so, until quite tender and silky—you don't want any browning here. Stir in the leeks and garlic and cook for another few minutes, until the leeks soften up. Stir in the beans and wine. Add water or broth to cover the beans and bring just to a gentle simmer for a couple of minutes. Just before serving, stir in the reserved fennel wedges and any reserved fennel fronds. Top each bowl with any or all of the following: plenty of crumbled feta, chopped olives, and a squeeze from a lemon wedge.

Easy Little Rye Bread

rye flour * rolled oats * yeast

I found a dead-simple yeast bread recipe a couple of years back. It made its way into my kitchen, cozied up, and never left. It was deep in a cookbook inspired by the notebooks of Dulcie May Booker—a wonderful Kiwi home cook born nearly a century ago. Her bread, made with a blend of white flour, whole wheat flour, and rolled oats, is simple, unassuming, and a good friend to a slab of salted butter. I sometimes switch up the flours a bit, and this version is a common variation I make—particularly when there's rye flour left to use up. If you don't have rye flour, trade in an equal amount of whole wheat flour.

MAKES 1 LOAF

1½ cups | 360 ml warm water (105°F to 115°F | 41°C to 46°C)

1 packet (2 teaspoons | 7 g) active dry yeast

1 tablespoon runny honey

1 cup | 4.5 oz | 125 g unbleached all-purpose flour

1 cup | 5 oz | 140 g rye flour

1 cup | 3.5 oz | 100 g rolled oats (not instant oats)

1½ teaspoons fine-grain sea salt

2 tablespoons unsalted butter, melted, plus more for serving

Place the warm water into a bowl, sprinkle the yeast over top, and stir until the yeast dissolves. Stir in the honey; set aside for 5 to 10 minutes, until the yeast blooms and swells. Meanwhile, mix the all-purpose flour, rye flour, oats, and salt in a large bowl. Add the wet mixture to the dry and stir until everything comes together into a uniform dough.

Brush an 8-cup | 1.9L loaf pan generously with some of the melted butter. Turn the dough into the pan, cover with a clean, slightly damp cloth, and set to rise in a warm place for 30 minutes.

Preheat the oven to 350°F | 180°C. When ready, bake the bread for 35 to 40 minutes, until the loaf is golden and is pulling away from the sides of the pan. Finish things up by brushing the top of the loaf with the remaining melted butter, then slip the bread under the broiler for just a heartbeat—to give the top a bit of deeper color. Remove from the oven and quickly turn the bread out of the pan onto a rack to cool so it doesn't steam in the pan. Serve warm, slathered with butter and sprinkled with a bit of salt.

Red Lentil Hummus

whey ✳ black sesame ✳ lemon juice

This hummus is smooth as buttercream, in part because red lentils are used in place of the more typical chickpeas. Mung beans can be used an alternative base as well. Boost the hummus with a bit of whey, in place of water, for an added nutritional, probiotic kick. Red lentils lose much of their blush in the cooking process, but the resulting hummus is still a nice sight topped with chives and sesame.

MAKES ABOUT 3 CUPS | 680 G

2½ cups cooked red lentils (see Note)

2 medium cloves garlic

3 tablespoons freshly squeezed lemon juice

⅔ cup | 160 ml tahini

¾ teaspoon fine-grain sea salt

2 to 3 tablespoons whey (page 321), kefir, or warm water

2 teaspoons black sesame seeds

Extra-virgin olive oil, toasted sesame oil, minced chives, and/or chive blossoms, to serve

Start by adding the cooked lentils and garlic to a food processor and pulsing for at least a minute, scraping the paste from the corners once or twice along the way. Add the lemon juice, tahini, and sea salt. Blend again, another minute or so. Don't skimp on the blending time, but stop if the beans form a doughy ball inside the processor. At this point start adding the whey a splash at a time. Blend, blend, blend, until the hummus is smooth and light, aerated and creamy. Taste, and adjust to your liking—adding more lemon juice or salt, if needed. Serve topped with the black sesame seeds, and preferably, a good amount olive oil, a few drops of toasted sesame oil, lots of chives, and chive blossoms.

NOTE: Rinse 1½ cups | 9 oz | 255 g dried lentils well and place in a saucepan with 1¾ cups | 415 ml of water. Bring to a simmer, cover, and cook until tender, roughly 15 minutes.

Sprout Salad

avocado * almonds * mung bean sprouts * yogurt

I've included just a handful of recipes from my website, 101 Cookbooks, here, and this is one that made the cut. A powerhouse of a lunch salad, it comes together fast—fresh sprouted mung beans, creamy avocado, and golden, toasted almonds sit alongside a generous dollop of salted, arugula-spiked yogurt. It is beautiful, and you feel great eating it. If sprouts aren't your thing, know that you can easily swap in cooked mung beans, cannellini beans, or any lentils that hold their shape when cooked—black belugas or lentilles du Puy are both good options.

SERVES 2 TO 4

¾ cup | 6 oz | 170 g Greek-style yogurt

Fine-grain sea salt

1 handful of arugula, chopped

1 small bunch chives, minced, flowers (if any) reserved

8 oz | 225 g sprouted mung beans or cooked mung beans (about 2 cups)

A big handful of well-toasted sliced almonds

Good extra-virgin olive oil

1 ripe avocado, chopped

In a small bowl, combine the yogurt, ¼ teaspoon of salt, the arugula, and chives. In a larger bowl, toss the mung beans and almonds with a splash of olive oil and a pinch of salt. Add the avocado and gently toss once or twice more.

Serve the mung beans next to the yogurt mixture and drizzle with a bit more olive oil. If your bunch of chives included a few chive flowers, sprinkle them across the top.

Leek Soup

coconut milk * cauliflower * yuba skins * brown rice

*There are two ways to go
about making this soup—
using tendrils of yuba skins
if you have access to them,
and ribbons of egg pasta if
not. It's the sort of hearty
soup to make when the
weather is cold, or if you've
been overeager with leeks at
the market.*

SERVES 6

3 tablespoons extra-virgin olive or coconut oil

3 medium leeks, well washed and chopped

Zest of 2 lemons

9 cups | 2 L water

2½ teaspoons fine-grain sea salt

2 cups | 12 oz | 340 g cooked brown rice (page 309)

2 cups | 14 oz | 400 g cooked white beans (see page 306), or 1 (14-oz | 400g) can white beans, drained and rinsed

1 cup | 240 ml coconut milk

2 cups | 7.5 oz | 210 g cauliflower florets

5 oz | 140 g wide ribbon yuba skins or egg pasta

½ cup | 2 oz | 55 g chopped, toasted hazelnuts

Chives, dill, and/or lemon olive oil, to serve

In a large soup pan over medium-high heat, add the oil. When hot, stir in the leeks. Sauté, stirring regularly, until the leeks soften and take on a bit of color, about 7 minutes. Stir in the zest of one lemon, wait another minute, then add the water and salt and bring to a simmer. Stir in the rice, beans, and coconut milk and let everything come back up to a simmer. Add the cauliflower and yuba skins, simmer for another minute or so, and serve in bowls, diving deep into the pot to include lots of good chunks in each bowl. Serve topped with more lemon zest, toasted hazelnuts, chives, dill, and a final drizzle of oil (or lemon-infused olive oil if you have some on hand).

Yellow Wax Beans

microscallions ✴ pepitas ✴ avocado ✴ clarified butter

The sort of quick and easy side I love. When you come across them, snatch up yellow wax beans for their crispy juiciness and strong flavor, but know that good green beans will be great too, or another structured seasonal vegetable like asparagus, broccoli, or cauliflower.

SERVES 4

12 oz | 340 g yellow wax beans

2 tablespoons clarified butter (see page 315)

¼ cup | 0.75 oz | 25 g sliced almonds

¼ cup | 1 oz | 35 g pepitas

Fine-grain sea salt

A handful of finely minced green onions, or use microscallions

Generous sprinkling of za'atar (see page 318) or fresh herbs

½ ripe avocado, thinly sliced

Trim the ends of the beans and slice into 1-inch | 2.5cm pieces.

Heat the clarified butter in a large skillet over medium-high heat. Stir in the almonds and pepitas along with a pinch of salt. Cook, stirring often, until golden. Add the beans, toss to coat, cover, and cook for a couple of minutes, just long enough for the beans to get a bit tender. Transfer to a serving bowl, sprinkle with the onions and za'atar, and arrange the sliced avocado at the side.

Shredded Tofu Stir-Fry (page 34)

Shredded Tofu Stir-Fry

serrano chile ∗ toasted pepitas ∗
pea shoots ∗ black sesame

This snappy little stir-fry comes together in a flash. You get freshness from bright pea shoots, substance from tofu, and some crunch from the pepitas and sesame seeds. It's an easy crowd-pleaser. You'll need to use a box grater for this; finer Microplane graters will shred the tofu too thinly to maintain structure. Leftovers are a favored spring roll filling as well.

(Pictured on the
previous pages.)

SERVES 4

1 small serrano chile,
seeded and minced

Fine-grain sea salt

1 tablespoon white wine
vinegar

1 teaspoon runny honey

4 tablespoons | 60 ml extra-
virgin olive oil

1 tablespoon crème fraîche,
buttermilk, or sour
cream

2 cups | 2 oz | 55 g pea
shoots

8 oz | 225 g extra-firm tofu,
shredded on a box grater

½ cup | 2.5 oz | 70 g well-
toasted pepitas

3 tablespoons black
sesame seeds

Start by making the dressing; you'll want it ready when you start to cook. Whisk together the chile, ¼ teaspoon of salt, the vinegar, honey, and 3 tablespoons of the olive oil, until emulsified. Add the crème fraîche and whisk again. Taste and adjust to your liking. Set aside.

Just before serving, heat the remaining tablespoon of olive oil in a large skillet or wok over medium-high heat. When hot, add the pea shoots and a pinch of salt and sauté for just 5 seconds or so. The shoots will quickly begin to wilt. Immediately transfer them to a plate and place the tofu in the hot skillet with most of the pepitas and sesame seeds and two-thirds of the dressing. Turn off the heat and toss gently to distribute the ingredients without breaking down the tofu too much—you just want to warm the mixture a bit. Taste and stir in more salt if needed. Transfer to a serving platter and top with the pea shoots and remaining sesame seeds and pepitas. Serve the extra dressing on the side.

Spring Carrots & Beans

lemon ⁕ shallots ⁕ dill ⁕ brown sugar

Warm, coin-shaped slices of golden, pan-fried carrots, white beans, and chopped dill tossed with a tangy-sweet lemon shallot dressing make this a compelling preparation. It tastes good the day you make it, even better the day after. And though it's certainly not as pretty, in my opinion it might taste best on day three, as the shallots infuse the beans, and the lemon mellows and deepens. I like to buy young carrots at the farmers' market: slice them slightly thicker than a banana chip here.

(Pictured on the following pages.)

SERVES 6 TO 8

¼ cup | 60 ml extra-virgin olive oil

3 tablespoons freshly squeezed lemon juice

¼ teaspoon fine-grain salt

½ cup | 2.5 oz | 70 g thinly sliced shallots

Olive oil or clarified butter (see page 315), for cooking

2 cups | 7.5 oz | 210 g sliced carrots, cut ¼ inch | 6 mm thick on the diagonal

3 cups | 20 oz | 565 g cooked white beans

¼ cup | 0.25 oz | 7 g chopped fresh dill

2 tablespoons brown sugar or honey

⅓ cup | 1 oz | 30 g sliced almonds, toasted

Combine the olive oil, lemon juice, salt, and shallots in a small bowl. Stir and set aside.

In your largest skillet over medium-high heat, toss the carrots with a splash of olive oil or a spoonful of clarified butter. Let them cook in a single layer. They'll give off a bit of water at first; keep cooking, tossing gently every 3 or 4 minutes until the carrots are deeply browned. All told, about 12 minutes.

Add the beans and dill to the skillet and cook, stirring often, for another 5 minutes, until the beans are heated through. If you are using beans that weren't canned, you can allow them to brown a bit as well, cooking a bit longer and stirring less frequently—they can handle this in a way that most canned beans can't. If you need to add a bit more oil to the pan to keep things from sticking, do so.

Place the contents of the skillet in a large mixing bowl, sprinkle with the brown sugar, and pour three-quarters of the lemon–olive oil mixture over the top. Toss gently. Let sit for 10 minutes. Toss once again, taste, and adjust with more salt or sugar or lemon juice if needed to balance the flavors. Serve warm or at room temperature; finish by sprinkling with almonds just before serving.

Fregola Sarda

endive * toasted hazelnut * capers *
basil * hard-boiled eggs

Our neighborhood market stocks a particularly tasty brand of fregola, the tiny Sardinian pasta made from hard durum wheat flour—rolled, sun-dried, and toasted to a mix of shades of yellow, gold, and brown. The pasta is rustic and nutty, each grain with a raggy surface adept at catching flavor. Tossed with ribbons of endive, toasted hazelnuts, capers, and basil, this pasta makes a wonderful shoulder season recipe to consider as summer is winding down and the last of the basil is at the market.

SERVES 4 TO 6

3 large eggs

Fine-grain sea salt

1¼ cups | 7 oz | 200 g fregola

¼ cup | 60 ml extra-virgin olive oil

¼ cup | 1.5 oz | 45 g capers, rinsed and patted dry

1 medium clove garlic, smashed

1 lemon

2 or 3 medium endives, cored and cut into ½-inch | 1.25cm ribbons

½ cup | 0.5 oz | 15 g torn fresh basil

⅓ cup | 1.5 oz | 45 g chopped toasted hazelnuts

Place the eggs in a pot and cover with cold water by ½ inch | 1.2 cm or so. Bring to a gentle boil. Turn off the heat, cover, and let sit for exactly 10 minutes. Have a big bowl of ice water ready and when the eggs are done cooking, place them in the ice bath for 3 minutes or so—long enough to stop the cooking. Peel, grate on a box grater, toss with a couple pinches of salt, and set aside.

Bring at least 8 cups | 2 L of water to a boil, salt the water generously, add the fregola, and cook for 10 to 15 minutes (or follow the package instructions). You want it al dente, not at all mushy. Drain, rinse lightly with cold water, and shake off as much residual moisture as possible.

While the pasta is cooking, heat the olive oil in a large skillet over medium-high heat. Add the capers and garlic and cook until the capers burst and start to brown. Remove from the heat, discard the garlic, and stir in ¼ teaspoon of salt.

To serve, transfer the fregola to a large bowl or platter. Pour the contents of the skillet on top of the pasta and give it a good toss. Add the zest from the lemon and about 1½ tablespoons of lemon juice—a good, generous squeeze. Add the endives, basil, and most of the hazelnuts and toss again. Taste and adjust seasoning before finishing with the grated eggs and the remaining hazelnuts.

Cold Soba Noodles

coriander seeds * paprika * toasted sesame

A favorite side project of mine is a little online culinary boutique named QUITOKEETO. No matter how many boxes there are to ship or honey jars to be wrapped, we always clear the packing table, take a break, and sit down for a proper lunch. This was an early favorite—cold soba noodles, tiny radishes (and greens), and a beautiful crushed sesame, fresh coriander seeds, and paprika drizzle. Radish sprouts (or other sprouts) in place of the sliced radishes are a fine substitution. Use fresh coriander seeds if you come across them late in summer at your local farmers' market; otherwise substitute dried. If using dried coriander seeds, toast them in a dry skillet until fragrant before using.

SERVES 4

Fine-grain sea salt

8 oz | 225 g dried soba noodles

¾ cup | 5 oz | 140 g slivered breakfast radishes, tops reserved

1 medium shallot, thinly sliced

¼ cup | 60 ml brown rice wine vinegar

1 small clove garlic

1 tablespoon toasted sesame seeds, plus more for serving

1½ teaspoons fresh or dried coriander seeds

1 teaspoon runny honey

½ cup | 120 ml extra virgin olive oil

½ teaspoon sweet paprika

⅛ teaspoon smoked paprika

Bring a large pot of water to a boil, salt, and cook the soba noodles per the package instructions. Drain and rinse under cold water until cool. In the meantime, place the radishes in a small bowl, toss with ⅛ teaspoon of salt, and set aside. Place the shallot in a separate small bowl with the vinegar and ⅛ teaspoon of salt. Set this aside as well.

Place the garlic in a mortar, sprinkle with ½ teaspoon of salt, and mash into a paste with the pestle. Add the sesame and coriander seeds and pound into a paste. Work in the honey and olive oil very gradually, then both paprikas. Blend until uniform.

To serve, place the soba noodles in large bowl along with the radishes. Stem the radish tops, and if they look good, slice into a chiffonade (you'll get about ½ cup) before adding to the bowl. Add the shallot and vinegar mixture and toss. Drizzle with the sesame-paprika paste, toss well, and garnish with a generous sprinkle of sesame seeds. Taste and season with more salt or honey if needed.

OPTIONAL: Serve topped with soft-poached eggs or an omelet sliced into a whispery-thin chiffonade.

Mashed Yellow Split Peas

shallots ✻ sea salt

This side dish started as a dumpling filling one night—mashed yellow split peas heavily flecked with caramelized shallots, thinned with a bit of coconut milk. The discovery was that everyone liked it on its own—think of it as a high-protein alternative to mashed potatoes.

SERVES 4

2 cups | 11 oz | 310 g cooked yellow split peas

⅓ cup | 80 ml coconut milk

Fine-grain sea salt

⅓ to ¾ cup | 80 to 180 ml warm water

3 tablespoons sunflower oil or clarified butter (see page 315)

1 cup | 4 oz | 115 g thinly sliced medium shallots (about 8)

Place the split peas in a food processor and pulse until dry and fluffy. Add the coconut milk and ½ teaspoon of salt and pulse a bit. Add the warm water, a small amount at a time, stopping when the split peas are creamy and light. Set aside. (You might want to transfer them to a saucepan or oven to warm.)

In a large skillet over medium heat, fry the shallots in the sunflower oil with a pinch of salt until golden brown, 7 minutes or so. Stir half the shallots into the split peas along with half the residual oil from the skillet. Serve the pureed split peas drizzled with any remaining oil and shallots.

Spicy Green Soup

serrano chile * herbs * ginger * almonds

I was at Bar Tartine for dinner one evening, and a man at the table next to me was hunched over a beautiful bowl of electric green fisherman's stew. He took in the scent wafting up from the shallow bowl for ten seconds before raising his spoon to take a first bite. I thought a lot about the impression that soup made. Not just on him, but on me, and seemingly everyone in the vicinity—the color, the fragrance, the rustic simplicity of the bowl—it made me want to make a soup with a kindred spirit.

I chipped away at this restorative, herb-forward, spicy, vegetarian version in the following months. Serve over poached eggs, giant beans, brown rice, or any of a range of noodles, and don't skimp on the toppings—they're part of what makes the whole preparation special.

SERVES 4 TO 6

4 cups | 1 L water

3 medium cloves garlic

¾ cup firmly packed | 0.75 oz | 20 g basil leaves

1¼ cups firmly packed | 1.25 oz | 35 g cilantro leaves and stems

¼ cup lightly packed | 0.25 oz | 7 g mint leaves

A thick 2-inch | 5cm piece of ginger, peeled and sliced

3 tablespoons extra-virgin olive oil

2 small serrano chiles, stemmed

½ cup | 1.5 oz | 45 g sliced almonds

1 teaspoon fine-grain sea salt

Zest of 1 lemon

1 tablespoon runny honey

Poached eggs (page 320), hot white beans, soba noodles, or brown rice (page 309), to serve (optional)

Chopped black olives, lemon wedges, toasted almonds, shaved green onions, or roasted, sliced mushrooms (or other oven-roasted vegetable), to top

In a saucepan, bring the water just to a simmer. As the water heats, combine the garlic, basil, cilantro, mint, ginger, olive oil, chiles, almonds, salt, lemon zest, and honey in a blender or food processor. Process for a couple of minutes, thinning with a couple of tablespoons of cold water and scraping down the sides along the way, until the mixture becomes as smooth as possible. Taste and adjust to your liking; the paste should taste strong and spicy. Just before serving, add the paste to the simmering water and stir well. Dial back the heat at this point; you don't want it to return to a simmer, but you do want it very hot. Taste and adjust the seasoning—a bit more salt or a squeeze of lemon juice. Ladle into bowls with your chosen accompaniment and enjoy on its own or topped with any of the suggested toppings.

Edamame Mint Spread

smoked almonds ✳ fresh mint ✳ black pepper

This is one of those hand-me-down recipes—a friend gives it to a friend and somehow it makes it to you because it is that good— everyone making his or her own tweaks along the way. I encountered a version of this salad when my friend Sarah Lonsdale brought it to a beautiful al fresco vineyard lunch on a sunny afternoon in Napa. It was her take on an Eric Gower recipe. This is my version.

A few tips: Smoked nuts can be tricky to find. Instead, I often use regular unsmoked almonds and smoked salt (in place of the sea salt called for) to develop the desired flavor. Also, don't skimp on the black pepper. The secret here is getting the balance of flavors right, and truth be told, I spend as much time doing that as making the spread itself. Serve over sesame-oiled soba noodles or brown rice, and you have a meal.

SERVES 4 TO 6

1½ cups | 9 oz | 255 g shelled edamame

½ cup | 2 oz | 55 g whole smoked almonds

1 cup lightly packed | 1 oz | 30 g mint leaves

1 large clove garlic

⅔ cup | 160 ml extra-virgin olive oil

Fine-grain sea salt

Freshly ground black pepper

Freshly squeezed lemon juice

Cook the edamame in a pot of boiling salted water, for just 30 seconds, and drain. Pulse the edamame, almonds, mint, garlic, olive oil, and ½ teaspoon of salt in a food processor six or seven times, aiming for chunks the size of pencil shavings. Transfer about half of the mixture to a serving bowl and pulse the remaining mixture a few more times before adding it to the bowl as well. Season with generous amounts of both black pepper and lemon juice to taste—really go for it, stirring to combine along the way.

Stir-Fry for Grace

tofu ✳ asparagus ✳ lemon verbena ✳ serrano chile

One of my favorite cooking vessels is a hand-pounded cast-iron wok I purchased alongside Grace Young in San Francisco's Chinatown. There are few people more knowledgeable or enthusiastic about traditional wok cooking than Grace, and she was nice enough to come over one afternoon to help put my baby wok through its initial paces. We made two stir-fries that afternoon, and this was one of them—simple, bright, and fresh with market asparagus and lemon verbena from a window box of herbs. Although lemon verbena can be tricky to come by, it adds an unexpected and fragrant green citrus note here. If you're having trouble sourcing it, feel free to swap in basil, shiso, and/or mint.

SERVES 2 OR 3

1 to 2 tablespoons sunflower oil or clarified butter (see page 315)

1 teaspoon grated ginger

1 clove garlic, minced

2 small shallots, chopped

1 small serrano chile, seeded and minced

8 to 10 oz | 170 to 285 g firm tofu, cut into thin slabs

6 to 8 oz | 170 to 225 g thin asparagus, cut into 1-inch | 2.5cm segments

1 tablespoon soy sauce

12 fresh lemon verbena leaves, shredded

Fine-grain sea salt and freshly ground pepper (optional)

Make sure all your ingredients are prepped and at the ready, because this will go fast. Heat a wok or large skillet over high heat until a drop of water vaporizes in a second or two. Swirl in 1 tablespoon of the oil and add the ginger, garlic, shallots, and chile pepper. Stir-fry for 20 or 30 seconds, or until fragrant and softened a bit.

Stir in the tofu and cook until it takes on a bit of color, adding a bit more oil at this point if needed. Now add the asparagus, all the while pushing the ingredients around the pan. Swirl in the soy sauce and continue to toss the ingredients. Finish with most of the lemon verbena, then taste and work in more soy sauce if needed (or perhaps a bit of salt and pepper instead). Quickly turn out onto a platter to serve; sprinkle generously with the remaining lemon verbena.

Salt-Baked Sweet Potato

olives * turmeric * grapefruit * dill * onion

I sometimes make this with massive russet potatoes, and other times—like this— with plump sweet potatoes: white-fleshed Japanese sweet potatoes are my preference. In either case, it's all about the toppings. The silky turmeric onions are good on just about anything, but particularly nice mingling with bursts of grapefruit segments, toasted walnuts, herbs, and crème fraîche. It's a quirky mix that somehow works.

SERVES 6

3 medium sweet potatoes

Large-grain sea salt

2 tablespoons extra virgin olive oil

1 medium yellow onion, quartered and thinly sliced

½ tablespoon turmeric

¼ teaspoon fine-grain sea salt

1 tablespoon white wine vinegar

Grapefruit segments, toasted walnuts, chopped olives, dill, chives, and arugula, to serve

½ cup | 120 ml crème fraîche

Preheat the oven to 400°F | 200°C. Scrub the sweet potatoes, prick them all over with a fork, and sprinkle generously with large-grain sea salt. Bake the sweet potatoes until tender throughout. This can take an hour for large potatoes, less for smaller.

While the potatoes are roasting, heat the olive oil in a skillet over medium heat. Add the onion, turmeric, and fine salt and cook until soft but not browned, about 7 minutes. Add the vinegar to the pan and let it caramelize for a minute or so, adding a couple of tablespoons of water if the pan becomes dry. Remove from the heat and set aside.

Next, prepare the toppings so they're ready when the hot sweet potatoes come out of the oven. When the potatoes are done, cut each in half lengthwise. Salt a bit and use a fork to gently fluff some of each half's flesh. Add a touch of crème fraîche, then really pile on the toppings and salt to taste. Serve nestled together in a bowl or on a platter with some arugula tucked about.

Pozole Verde

green chiles ✳ garlic ✳ cilantro ✳ oregano

Kernels of blossoming corn immersed in an intense green chile and roasted vegetable make this pozole special. It is based loosely on a Rancho Gordo recipe, and I make a point to serve it a few times during the summer when tomatillos are in season. There is a lady at the farmers' market who taught me to choose the smallest tomatillos, preferably with a blush of purple. You want fruit that is free from blemishes with the paper lantern still mostly intact. Those have the best flavor. When I can't get tomatillos, swapping in an equivalent amount of zucchini works brilliantly. You can cook pozole days or weeks ahead of time. Drained well, it freezes incredibly.

SERVES 6

8 oz | 225 g dried pozole (whole dried hominy)

Fine-grain sea salt

2 medium white onions, quartered

1 medium red onion, quartered

7 medium cloves garlic

4 tiny tomatillos, paper skins removed, rinsed

4 poblano chiles

2 serrano chiles

¼ cup | 60 ml extra-virgin olive oil

2 cups | 2 oz | 60 g coarsely chopped cilantro leaves and stems

1 tablespoon dried Mexican oregano

5 to 6 cups | 1.2 to 1.5 L water or broth reserved from cooking pozole, or good-tasting vegetable broth

Tortilla chips, toasted pepitas, queso fresco or feta, avocado, and/ or freshly cracked black pepper, to serve

Soak the pozole overnight in water to cover generously, as you would for dried beans. When you're ready to cook the pozole, drain and place it in a large saucepan covered with a few inches of water. Stir in 1 tablespoon of salt, add 4 white onion quarters, and bring to a simmer. Cover partially and cook at a gentle simmer until the kernels are tender and most of them have popped or blossomed— usually around 2 hours, sometimes longer. Remove from the heat and allow to cool in the cooking liquid. Drain, reserving the cooking liquid if you like, and set aside.

In the meantime, heat a large, dry griddle or skillet over medium-high heat and roast the remaining white and red onion quarters, the garlic, tomatillos, and chiles, turning often, until they are charred and slightly softened, 15 to 20 minutes. (An outdoor grill makes quick work of this as well.) Place the roasted chiles in a closed paper bag or tightly covered bowl to steam until cool. Transfer the other vegetables to a large glass bowl to cool, collecting any juices. Peel the garlic cloves and add them to the bowl. When cool, peel the poblanos, discarding the seeds and stems. Discard the serrano chile stems but don't skin or seed them. Add the chiles to the bowl of vegetables and use a hand blender to puree until smooth.

Heat the olive oil in a large stockpot over medium heat. Add the vegetable puree and ½ teaspoon of salt and adjust the heat to maintain a simmer. Cook, stirring occasionally, for 10 minutes to blend the flavors. Remove from the heat, add the cilantro and oregano and 1 cup | 240 ml of the water or broth, and immediately puree with the hand blender. Add 4 cups | 1 L more of water or broth. Add the pozole to the pot, thin with more broth if you like, taste, and season with more salt if needed. Bring back to a simmer and serve in warm bowls topped with tortilla chips, pepitas, queso fresco, avocado, and/or pepper.

Squash & Wild Rice Soup

winter squash ⁕ serrano chile ⁕ lemon ginger rosemary butter

Keep in mind that this soup is all about the lemon ginger rosemary butter playing off the nuttiness of the wild rice and the smoothness of the winter squash. The flair, in this case, is what makes it a soup worth sharing. Start with a winter squash roughly 4 pounds | 1.8 kg in weight—rugosa squash, or the unusual antique-blue triamble, are worth seeking out, but acorn and butternut are easy to come by and delicious as well.

SERVES 4 TO 6

LEMON GINGER ROSEMARY BUTTER

½ cup | 4 oz | 115 g unsalted butter

Chopped leaves from a 4-inch | 10cm sprig rosemary

Zest of 1 lemon

1 teaspoon grated ginger

Scant ¼ teaspoon fine-grain sea salt

¼ cup | 2 oz | 55 g unsalted butter

2 medium onions, cut into eighths

2 large shallots, halved

1 whole serrano chile, stemmed

1 tablespoon fine-grain sea salt

2½ pounds | 1.1 kg pumpkin or squash, seeded, peeled, and cut into ¾-inch | 2cm chunks

9 cups | 2 L water

2 teaspoons fresh ginger juice (page 316)

2 to 4 cups | 10 to 20 oz | 300 to 600 g warm cooked wild rice, to serve

Plain yogurt and toasted pepitas, to serve

To make the lemon ginger rosemary butter, heat the butter in a small saucepan over medium heat for about 3 minutes—long enough for it to start to brown a bit. Remove from the heat and immediately stir in the rosemary, lemon zest, grated ginger, and salt. Stir well and let sit for 5 minutes or so. Strain the butter and reserve the pulp to serve separately.

To make the soup, melt the butter in a large soup pot over medium-high heat. Add the onions, shallots, serrano, and salt. Cook until softened, about 5 minutes, then add the pumpkin and the water (less if you like a thicker soup, though this soup is nice on the thinner side). Bring just to a simmer and cook until the squash is completely tender throughout, about 15 minutes. Note that the time it takes will differ among different squash varietals. Remove from the heat, puree with a hand blender until smooth, and stir in the ginger juice. If you like an even thinner soup, add a bit more water at this point, then stir in more salt to taste.

Serve over a big scoop of wild rice with a dollop of yogurt, some pepitas, the lemon ginger rosemary butter, and a bit of pulp.

59

Mung Bean Stew

caraway ⁎ turmeric ⁎ smoked paprika ⁎ cilantro

Big spice. Big stew. My thought is, if you're going to bother assembling an ambitious list of spices like this, you might as well make a sizeable pot, with the potential for leftovers for days. Here you have hearty, filling mung beans and farro rounded out with a blend of earthy, nutritionally punchy, warming spices. Cooled, it is a stew that freezes well. While I call for semipearled farro, brown rice works equally well.

SERVES 8

½ cup | 120 ml olive oil

6 celery stalks, chopped

1 medium onion, chopped

1 teaspoon caraway seed

1 teaspoon whole coriander seeds

1 teaspoon whole anise seeds

5 whole cloves

3 medium cloves garlic, sliced paper-thin

1¼ teaspoons fine-grain sea salt

¾ teaspoon ground turmeric

½ teaspoon red pepper flakes

¾ teaspoon ground cinnamon

1 teaspoon smoked paprika

3 cups | 21 oz | 600 g cooked mung beans

2 cups | 12 oz | 340 g cooked semipearled farro

4 cups | 1 L water or good-tasting vegetable broth

Lots of chopped cilantro and/or salted plain yogurt, to serve

Heat the olive oil in a large soup pot over medium-high heat. Stir in the celery and onion and sauté, stirring every few minutes, until the celery starts to take on a bit of color.

While the celery mixture is cooking, grind the caraway, coriander, anise, and cloves to a sandy texture in a mortar and pestle. Add this spice mixture, along with the garlic, to the celery and sauté for a couple of minutes, until the garlic softens a bit. Stir in the salt, turmeric, red pepper flakes, cinnamon, and paprika. Stir well and allow to cook for another minute or so, long enough for the spices to get fragrant and toasted. Stir in the mung beans and farro and then the water. You should have enough liquid in the pot to cover the other ingredients—go ahead and add a bit more if needed. Bring to a simmer and cook for at least 10 minutes. Taste and add more salt if needed. Serve topped with lots of cilantro and dollops of yogurt.

Cauliflower Pasta

za'atar ✳ crème fraîche ✳ green olives

This mixture of cauliflower florets, za'atar, and crème fraîche can be served over strips of yuba skins cut into pappardelle shape, or over traditional pasta—thin, flat egg noodles are best. The olives are important: plump, buttery Castelvetrano olives are great if you can find them, but any medium-large good-tasting green olives will do—just not from a can.

SERVES 4 TO 6

8 oz | 225 g yuba skins or dried pasta

1½ to 3 tablespoons extra-virgin olive oil

Fine-grain sea salt

12 oz | 340 g cauliflower, cut into small florets

15 green olives, rinsed, smashed, pitted, and chopped

3 tablespoons crème fraîche, plus more for serving

2 teaspoons za'atar (see page 318)

If you're using yuba skins, cut them into ½-inch | 1.2cm strips and separate the "noodles" into single layers, creating a light, airy tangle of yuba. Heat 1½ tablespoons of the olive oil in a large skillet over medium-high heat and pan-fry the yuba with a generous pinch of salt for about 7 minutes, until the edges of the yuba take on nice amount of color and crisp up some. Remove from the pan and set aside. (Alternatively, if you're using pasta, cook according to the package instructions in well-salted water. Drain and set aside.)

To cook the cauliflower, heat the remaining 1½ table-spoons of olive oil in the same skillet over medium-high heat. Add the cauliflower and a pinch of salt and sauté, stirring occasionally, until the edges brown. About 30 seconds before you think the cauliflower will be cooked, stir in the olives. Remove from the heat, wait about 10 seconds, then stir in the crème fraîche. Serve over the bed of yuba skins or noodles, either on individual plates or family-style, sprinkled generously with za'atar and drizzled with crème fraîche.

Cara Cara Chop Salad

toasted garlic * peanuts * celery * herbs

*This recipe is an example
of how toasted garlic can
be used as punctuation.
It is a winter salad that
has a lot going for it—
juicy sweetness from
the oranges, the crunchy
saltiness of the peanuts,
refreshing flecks of mint,
and the crispness of celery,
all tangled within a bed
of wilted radicchio. To turn
it into a meal, serve it over
cold bean thread noodles
or a bed of brown rice. It's
also a recipe that comes
together nicely in a wok
instead of skillet.*

SERVES 4 TO 6

¼ cup | 60 ml freshly
squeezed lime juice

¼ teaspoon fine-grain
sea salt

⅛ teaspoon freshly ground
black pepper

½ tablespoon honey

2 tablespoons extra-virgin
olive oil

1 tablespoon chopped
garlic

4 cups | 5 oz | 140 g chopped
radicchio

1 cup | 4 oz | 115 g celery
cut on the diagonal into
½-inch | 1.2cm pieces

¼ cup | 0.25 oz | 8 g
chopped chives

1 cup | 6 oz | 170 g Cara Cara
orange segments, halved

½ cup | 0.5 oz | 15 g torn
mint leaves

1 cup | 4 oz | 115 g peanuts,
toasted and coarsely
chopped

Start by assembling the dressing. Stir together the lime
juice, salt, black pepper, and honey. Set aside.

In a large skillet over medium heat, add the olive oil and
garlic, then carefully tilt the pan to pool the oil and toast
the garlic. When the garlic begins to color uniformly, after
a couple of minutes, turn off the heat—medium toasted is
what you're after, not burnt. With a slotted spoon, remove
the toasted garlic to a paper towel and allow it to cool completely, reserving the garlic oil in the skillet. Using the
same pan, dial the heat up a bit more, and when the oil is
hot, add the chopped radicchio. Stir every 10 seconds or so
until the radicchio is lightly wilted but still crunchy, about
1 minute total. Remove from the pan. Just before serving,
combine the celery, chives, orange segments, mint, and
peanuts—reserving a bit of each for finishing—on a large
platter or in a bowl. Add the radicchio, toasted garlic,
and dressing to the bowl and toss to coat. Finish with the
reserved celery, chives, oranges, mint, and peanuts.

Rye Pound Cake

rye flour ✳ seed medley ✳ caraway ✳ orange zest

Baking in earthenware molds is wonderful—the thick walls allow steady, gentle heat to permeate your batter, and they're often beautiful enough to serve cakes in. Keep your eyes peeled at flea markets and yard sales for unusual shapes and sizes. I bake this beauty in my favorite Bundt pan. Made with 100 percent rye flour, it is a tender-crumbed, highly seeded, unfussy affair. Able to work on both sweet and savory fronts, it's the sort of cake that is at home as part of a brunch or picnic or sliced alongside a cheese plate.

MAKES 1 CAKE

2¼ cups | 10 oz | 285 g rye flour

2 teaspoons aluminum-free baking powder

¾ teaspoon fine-grain sea salt

1 teaspoon lightly toasted caraway seeds

1½ tablespoons black sesame seeds

⅓ cup | 2 oz | 60 g sunflower seeds

1 cup | 4 oz | 115 g pepitas

1 tablespoon freshly grated orange zest

¾ cup | 6 oz | 170 g unsalted butter, at room temperature

1 cup | 7.5 oz | 215 g sifted natural cane or muscovado sugar

½ cup | 120 ml runny honey

2 teaspoons vanilla extract

3 eggs, at room temperature

1 cup | 240 ml full-fat yogurt

Preheat the oven to 350°F | 175°C. Butter the sides of a 10-cup | 2.5L Bundt pan (or equivalent), dust with flour, and set aside.

Combine the rye flour, baking powder, salt, caraway, sesame seeds, sunflower seeds, pepitas, and zest in a bowl. By hand, or using an electric mixer, combine the butter and sugar and beat until light and fluffy. Gradually beat in the honey and vanilla extract, then add the eggs one at a time, fully incorporating each into the mixture before adding the next. Add half of the flour mixture and mix until incorporated before mixing in half of the yogurt. Repeat with the remaining flour mixture and yogurt, scraping down the sides of the bowl a few times along the way. Pour the batter into the prepared pan, rap against the counter carefully to dislodge any air bubbles, and bake for 50 to 60 minutes, or until a tester inserted into the center of the pan comes out clean. Let sit for 5 minutes or so before turning out to cool on a baking rack; or serve in the pan.

Buttermilk Cakes

rye flour * vanilla * buttermilk glaze

These are cakes you can wrap in parchment and toss in a market bag, picnic sack, or carry-on. They're go-anywhere, unfussy, and charmingly simple treats, inspired by a buttermilk cake by Nikole Herriott that ran in Anthology *magazine a couple of years back. I've been doing a version with a good percentage of rye flour, which plays off the vanilla nicely. This recipe makes about 7½ cups | 1.75 L of batter, which I divide across three small, odd-sized pans—often charlotte molds or tiny Bundts, but feel free to play around. You might do one larger cake or a few smaller ones as shown here. For an entirely whole grain batter, you can substitute whole wheat pastry flour for the all-purpose flour for a more rustic final result.*

(Pictured on the following pages.)

MAKES 3 CAKES

2 cups | 8 oz | 225 g
   rye flour

2 cups | 9 oz | 255 g
   unbleached all-
   purpose flour

2 tablespoons aluminum-
   free baking powder

1 teaspoon fine-grain
   sea salt

2 cups | 480 ml buttermilk

2 teaspoons vanilla extract

1 cup | 8 oz | 225 g unsalted
   butter, at room
   temperature

1½ cups | 7.5 oz | 210 g
   natural cane sugar

4 eggs, at room
   temperature

BUTTERMILK GLAZE

1½ cups | 7 oz | 200 g
   organic confectioners'
   sugar

3 to 4 tablespoons
   buttermilk

1 vanilla bean, split
   and scraped

Preheat the oven to 350°F | 175°C. Butter and flour three small- to medium-size cake pans, tapping out any excess flour. You can use whatever pan or pans you like, just be mindful not to fill any of them more than two-thirds full before baking.

Sift the flours, baking powder, and salt into a bowl and set aside. In a separate bowl combine the buttermilk and vanilla and set aside.

Using a stand mixer with a paddle attachment, cream the butter until light and fluffy. With the machine on, add the sugar. Beat until well incorporated. Be sure to turn off the mixer and scrape down the sides once or twice at this stage. Add the eggs one at a time, incorporating each egg before the next addition. Mix until the batter is uniform, creamy, and billowy.

Either by hand or with the mixer on low, add one-third of the dry ingredients, then one-third of the buttermilk, stirring between each addition just enough to incorporate. Repeat until all of the dry and wet ingredients are in the batter, being mindful to avoid overmixing.

Divide the batter among the prepared pans, set the pans on a baking sheet, and bake until the cakes are golden-topped and spring back when you touch the top, usually 30 to 50 minutes: smaller cakes will bake more quickly than larger ones, Bundt pans more quickly than conventional pans. Pull each cake from the oven when it is properly baked and let cool in the pan a couple of minutes before turning out onto a cooling rack.

While the cakes are cooling, make the buttermilk glaze. Whisk together the confectioners' sugar, buttermilk, and vanilla seeds in a bowl until smooth (reserve the scraped pod for another use). Drizzle this glaze across the cakes, allowing it to flow across the tops and down the sides.

I tend to leave these cakes out on the counter for snacking, but you can also store them in an airtight container to keep them from drying out if they need to keep for more than a day.

Baked Oatmeal

pluots * kefir * almonds

I suspect the baked oatmeal recipe in my last book made it into more kitchens than any other recipe I've ever written. It's still a regular here at home, in various guises, and this is a version worth celebrating. Made with crimson-fleshed Dapple Dandy pluots, it rides the line beautifully between the sweetness of the summer fruit and the tanginess of the kefir or buttermilk. Other stone fruit can be substituted.

SERVES 6

Zest of 1 lemon

2 cups | 7 oz | 200 g rolled oats

½ cup | 2 oz | 60 g whole Marcona almonds

1 teaspoon aluminum-free baking powder

Scant ½ teaspoon fine-grain sea salt

⅓ cup | 2 oz | 60 g maple syrup, plus more for serving

1 cup | 240 ml kefir or buttermilk

1 cup | 240 ml water

1 egg

3 tablespoons unsalted butter, melted and cooled slightly

2 teaspoons pure vanilla extract

1 pound | 455 g ripe pluots, quartered and pitted

A bit of cream, to serve

Preheat the oven to 375°F | 190°C with a rack in the top third of the oven. Generously butter the inside of an 8-inch | 20cm square baking dish (or equivalent), then sprinkle with lemon zest.

In a bowl, mix together the oats, almonds, baking powder, and salt. In another bowl, whisk together the maple syrup, kefir, water, egg, half of the butter, and the vanilla. Arrange the pluots in a single layer in the bottom of the prepared baking dish. Cover the fruit with the oat mixture. Slowly drizzle the kefir mixture over the oats. Gently give the baking dish a couple of raps on the countertop to make sure the liquid moves through the oats.

Bake for 35 to 45 minutes, until the top is nicely golden and the oat mixture has set. Remove from the oven and let cool for a few minutes. Drizzle the remaining melted butter on the top and serve. Finish with a bit more maple syrup if you want it a bit sweeter, and a thread of cream to bring it all together.

Quinoa Blini

quinoa flour ✳ buttermilk

*Quinoa flour is worth
seeking out—you get
many of the nutritional
benefits of quinoa, in
flour form. I make these
tender, golden pancakes
at least once a week, often
for a speedy lunch, or as
part of a casual dinner.
They're unleavened, so a
bit different than a fluffy
American-style pancake;
approach them the way you
might a blini or tortilla—
consider topping with
smashed avocado, or salted
yogurt, or hot sauce. I'm
including a base recipe here,
but I often add seeds, spices,
and seasonings to the
batter. The batter keeps well
for 4 to 5 days refrigerated.
You can also make a great
version with chickpea flour
in place of the quinoa flour.*

MAKES ABOUT 20 BLINI

1½ cups | 6.75 oz | 190 g
quinoa flour

1¼ teaspoons fine-grain
sea salt

2 eggs

½ cup | 120 ml water

1 cup | 240 ml buttermilk
or yogurt

3 tablespoons melted
butter, clarified butter
(see page 315), or
coconut oil

Extra-virgin coconut oil
or clarified butter (see
page 315), for frying

1 teaspoon mustard seeds,
1 teaspoon ground
turmeric, 1 tablespoon
sesame seeds,
½ teaspoon chile flakes,
and/or crushed thyme
(optional)

Combine the quinoa flour, salt, eggs, water, buttermilk,
and butter. Whisk until the batter is smooth. You're after
a batter that is on the thin side, similar to a crepe batter.
Let it sit for 10 minutes if you have the time, allowing the
flour to absorb the liquids. Stir again.

Heat butter or coconut oil—just enough to coat the
pan—in a large skillet over medium heat. Ladle 2 to
3 tablespoons of batter per blini into the pan and cook for
approximately 3 minutes per side, or until lightly golden,
with crisped edges. Transfer from the pan to a paper towel
or clean kitchen towel and blot gently. Repeat with the
remaining batter, adding more fat to the pan as needed.

These are best enjoyed immediately, but you can also
place them on an ovenproof platter in a low-heat oven
while cooking the remaining pancakes, or wrap them in
a clean dish cloth. Alternately, a quick reheat in the skillet
just before serving brings them right back to life if they've
cooled off.

Frittata

turmeric ✳ saffron ✳ sesame ✳ salted yogurt

Frittatas are a classic family-style preparation, and a twelve-egg version is an easy addition to just about every brunch or breakfast I host. It takes minimal effort and provides a substantial protein-based option that contrasts with sweet, starchier morning options like muffins, waffles, or pancakes. Drizzled with a luxe saffron-turmeric butter and finished with lots of fresh herbs and salted yogurt, this version steps it up a notch. My cast-iron skillet is my preferred pan for frittatas, but any large, ovenproof pan will do.

SERVES 6 TO 8

4 tablespoons | 2 oz | 55 g unsalted butter, melted

1 pound | 455 g new potatoes, very thinly sliced

½ teaspoon fine-grain sea salt

12 large eggs, whisked

½ teaspoon ground turmeric

Zest of 1 lemon

1 pinch saffron (about 20 threads), crushed

1 serrano chile, seeded and minced

⅓ cups | 80 ml plain full-fat yogurt, salted to taste

1 tablespoon toasted sesame seeds

Chopped fresh basil, mint, and/or fennel fronds, to finish

Heat 1 tablespoon of the butter in an ovenproof 12-inch |30cm heavy skillet—preferably cast-iron—over medium-high heat. Stir in the potatoes and sprinkle with a bit of the salt. Cover and cook until the potatoes are tender, scraping along the bottom of the pan to stir occasionally, 5 to 10 minutes. Whisk the remaining salt into the eggs and pour the eggs into the skillet with the potatoes. Cook over medium-low heat for a few minutes, until the eggs are just set and there isn't a lot of liquid running around the pan. To facilitate this, run a spatula underneath the sides of the frittata and tilt the pan so the uncooked eggs run to the underside. The key is to avoid browning on the bottom.

Remove from the heat and place under the broiler for a couple of minutes, until the top of the frittata has puffed up and set. Remove from the broiler and let sit for a minute or two. In the meantime, warm the remaining butter with the turmeric, lemon zest, saffron, and chile.

Serve the frittata in the pan, warm or at room temperature, drizzled with the turmeric butter, dolloped with the salted yogurt, and sprinkled with the sesame seeds and fresh herbs.

Whole Wheat Waffles

whole wheat flour ✳ wheat germ ✳ buttermilk

These are the waffles I make most often—big and Belgian-style. A combination of flours and rolled oats is lightened up with a bit of rice flour or organic cornstarch. It is a blend that conspires with lots of buttermilk to give the waffles a nice, moist interior and a crisp, golden crust.

MAKES 16 BELGIAN-STYLE
WAFFLES

1 cup | 4.5 oz | 120 g whole wheat flour

2 cups | 9 oz | 255 g all-purpose flour

½ cup | 1.75 oz | 50 g rolled oats, or ½ cup | 1.5 oz | 40 g wheat germ

4 oz | 110 g organic cornstarch or rice flour

2 teaspoons fine-grain sea salt

2 teaspoons baking powder

1 teaspoon baking soda

4 cups | 1 L buttermilk

½ cup | 4 oz | 115 g butter, melted and cooled

4 eggs, separated

Preheat the oven to 225°F | 110°C. Combine the flours, oats, cornstarch, salt, baking powder, and baking soda in a large bowl. In a separate bowl, whisk together the buttermilk, melted butter, and egg yolks. In a third bowl, using an egg beater or an electric mixer, beat the egg whites into stiff peaks.

Heat the waffle maker, and when it is ready, add the buttermilk mixture to the dry ingredients and stir until the mixture just starts to come together. Dollop the egg whites across the top of the batter and fold until uniform, using as few strokes as possible.

Use a scoop to ladle the batter into your waffle iron and cook until deeply golden and crisp. Transfer to the warm oven while you make the remaining waffles—the dry heat of the oven helps them set a bit. Any leftover batter will keep for a day or so, refrigerated.

Lilikoi Curd

fresh passion fruit juice ✳ eggs ✳ Meyer lemon

Perfumed, acidic, complex, and intense, lilikoi—better known as passion fruit—is a heavenly flavor. There is a vendor who sells them at my market for what seems like a single, delicious, expensive, far-too-short month. I buy them heavy and let the fruit get wrinkly before using the juice to make curd. Compared to other curd recipes, this version goes relatively easy on the sweetener. Try it this way and feel free to adjust the sweetness in future batches based on the sweetness of your fruit and your general preference. If you don't have access to lilikoi, trade in other strong, strained fruit juice—raspberry, satsuma, and grapefruit are favorites of mine.

MAKES 1½ TO 2 CUPS | 360 TO 480 ML

12 passion fruit to yield ½ cup | 120 ml freshly squeezed passion fruit juice, strained

5 tablespoons | 2.5 oz | 70 g unsalted butter, at room temperature

⅓ cup | 2.5 oz | 70 g granulated sugar, or 3 tablespoons honey

2 egg yolks, at room temperature

2 eggs, at room temperature

⅛ teaspoon fine-grain sea salt

1 tablespoon freshly squeezed lemon juice, strained (preferably Meyer lemon)

Cut each passion fruit in half and scrape the pulp into a bowl with a spoon. Press through a strainer or cheesecloth to extract as much juice as possible, straining at the end if needed. You'll need ½ cup | 120 ml.

Cream the butter in a stainless steel bowl (note: you'll use this bowl as a makeshift double boiler later). Add the sugar and beat until fluffy and light. Add the yolks and then the eggs, one at a time, beating well to incorporate after each addition. Stir in the salt and then gradually add the passion fruit juice and the lemon juice, working the juice in as you go. Fill a small saucepan one-third of the way full with water. Bring to a simmer and place your stainless steel bowl of curd on top of it. Stir constantly and heat the curd slowly enough that the sugar (if you used it) has time to dissolve. This step should take about 10 minutes. Pull the curd from the heat when it is just thick enough to coat your spoon—a thermometer should top out at 166°F | 74°C (remember the temperature will continue to climb a bit off heat). Your curd will thicken substantially as it cools. There's no need to strain unless you somehow ended up with a few lumps (which you shouldn't). The curd will keep, refrigerated, for a week, and it's wonderful served warm or cold.

Ricotta Breakfast Bowl

honey * flower pepper * almonds * banana

I've received many notes from the Kennett Square, Pennsylvania, kitchen of my childhood friend Nikki Graham. They're typically short and often sum up something she's cooked for herself (or her family of six). I look forward to her ideas, because they're off-the-cuff and unfussy and often put ingredients together in a way I might not have thought about. This ricotta breakfast bowl is an example—substantial and a nice alternative to yogurt, and the addition of flower pepper gives it a beautiful kick. We both use the best quality whole milk ricotta we can find. Putting this bowl together is all about personal preference, so if you like more nutty crunch, go heavy on the almonds.

SERVES 1

½ banana, sliced

⅓ cup | 2.5 oz | 70 g good ricotta

Fine-grain sea salt

Drizzle of honey or chunk of honeycomb

Sprinkling of toasted sliced almonds

Dried fruit (golden raisins, sliced dates, or figs)

Flower pepper (page 312)

Arrange the banana slices to the side of the bowl. Season the ricotta with a bit of salt to your liking. Add the ricotta on the side of the bowl. Top with a drizzle of honey (or a chunk of honeycomb if you can get your hands on it), almonds, and dried fruit. Finish with plenty of flower pepper.

NOTE: I also regularly do a more savory version, drizzling the ricotta with good olive oil and sprinkling it generously with a mixture made from ⅓ cup | 1 oz | 30 g toasted almond slices ground in a mortar and pestle with a pinch of salt, a small garlic clove, and 8 whole coriander seeds.

Popovers

black pepper ✳ millet ✳ whole milk

Delightful and dramatic, popovers are an impressive addition to any baker's repertoire. Their crunchy exterior conceals a billowy, eggy interior that begs for a slather of butter or, my preference, ripe avocado. They're worth learning to make well—which, I'll be honest, takes a bit of practice. You need to make sure your oven has even, constant heat and good temperature control. A blast of heat in the beginning is needed to get an upward push going, then more gentle heat should be deployed to cook the popovers through, allowing a beautiful crust to develop. I use individual timbales here, but you can use a special popover pan or a muffin tin—the smoother and slipperier the sides, the better. Deep and narrow tins get great results, but muffin tins deliver the delight as well.

MAKES 6 TO 8 LARGE
POPOVERS, OR ABOUT
12 SMALLER ONES

2 cups | 475 ml whole milk

2 tablespoons unsalted butter

2 cups | 9 oz | 255 g whole wheat pastry flour or all-purpose flour

1¼ teaspoons fine-grain sea salt

¾ teaspoon non-aluminum baking powder

1½ teaspoons freshly ground black pepper

5 eggs, at room temperature

¼ cup | 1.5 oz | 45 g raw millet or sesame seeds

Start by preheating the oven to 425°F | 220°C, with a rack in the low center. Butter your pans, whether you are using individual timbales, popover pans, or a muffin tin. Place the pans on a baking sheet, preferably rimmed.

Combine the milk and butter in a saucepan and gently heat until the milk is warm to the touch, not more than 115°F | 45°C. Remove from the heat and set aside. Sift the flour, salt, and baking powder into a large bowl and stir in the black pepper. Set aside.

Now you're going to whisk the eggs. It's important to start with room-temperature eggs here, using an electric mixer with the whisk attachment at medium-high speed. It'll take a couple of minutes, but you want the eggs to get nice and voluminous and light, taking on the color of yellow taffy. Dial back the mixer speed and add the milk in a slow, steady stream. Gradually add the flour mixture a bit at a time and beat on medium speed for another 60 seconds. Transfer to a pitcher.

Preheat the empty popover pans in the oven for 3 minutes. Remove them carefully but quickly (you don't want to let all the heat from the oven) and fill each tin two-thirds full with batter. Sprinkle each popover with an equal amount of millet seeds. Transfer to the hot oven carefully (and quickly!) and dial back the heat to 400°F | 200°C. Bake for 30 to 45 minutes. I hate to give exact

times here—I really go by sight. Without opening the oven, I look for deep golden coloring on all sides and lots of airy lift. Bake as long as you can without letting the tops get too dark: if you let them bake on the long side, you'll end up with more structure, which helps keep the popovers puffed when they come out of the oven. When golden, remove, turn out onto a cooling rack, and enjoy as soon as possible.

Yogurt Bowl

pomegranate juice ✻ sunflower seeds ✻
puffed quinoa cereal

There were two or three other yogurt bowls contending for this spot. A summer beauty made with poppy seeds, pluots or plums, toasted oats, and honey. Another with persimmon, fennel or bee pollen, toasted oats, almonds, and almond extract. They were edged out by this, which is the one I think of most often and which was featured on my website a couple of years back. It's visually gorgeous and texturally interesting, with the smoothness of the yogurt punctuated with puffed quinoa and toasted sunflower seeds—a quick stunner at ease anchoring a brunch spread.

(Pictured on the following pages.)

SERVES 1

2 tablespoons fresh pomegranate juice

A drizzle of honey

A big dollop of Greek-style yogurt

A handful of puffed quinoa cereal

A sprinkling of toasted sunflower seeds

Whole pomegranate seeds or fresh or dried rose petals (optional)

A bit of bee pollen (optional)

In a bowl, swirl the pomegranate juice and honey into the yogurt just a bit, sprinkle with the cereal and sunflower seeds, then finish with the pomegranate seeds or rose petals and bee pollen (if you're using).

Strawberry Salad

toasted caraway ✳ brown sugar ✳ olive oil ✳ almonds

This salad is all about the berries—if the strawberries you come across aren't great, consider swapping in another soft fruit or berry. Served over Greek yogurt as part of a brunch or breakfast spread, the berries are jewel-like and perfect for adults and little ones.

SERVES 4 TO 6

1½ pounds | 680 g strawberries (about 2 baskets)

¾ teaspoon caraway seeds, lightly toasted

1½ tablespoons natural cane sugar or brown sugar

¼ teaspoon fine-grain sea salt

3 tablespoons extra-virgin olive oil

½ cup | 1.5 oz | 45 g sliced almonds, toasted

Zest of 1 lemon

Pick over the berries well, discarding any that are off. Brush away any dirt or debris with a damp cloth. Core and slice into quarters before placing in a large serving bowl.

Use a mortar and pestle to bruise the caraway seeds. Add the sugar and salt and grind a bit more to work the caraway into the sugar. Add the olive oil and stir to combine. If there is room in your mortar, use a spoon to stir in the almonds and lemon zest. If not, transfer to another bowl to combine.

Just before serving, pour most of the almond mixture over the berries. As gently as you can, mix together, folding and jostling the bowl to coat the strawberries. Do one last fold, top with the remaining nut mixture, and serve.

Turmeric Tea

turmeric ✳ black pepper ✳ honey ✳ lemon

A couple of years back, I wrote about a classic Ayurvedic turmeric paste I'd read about while paging through old cookbooks in the Los Angeles Library. Along with fresh lemon juice and a good jolt of black pepper, it is used as a healing, anti-inflammatory herbal tea base. The black pepper makes it invigorating (and also helps the body absorb the turmeric), and the honey sets off the earthy acridness of the spice enough to maintain the tea's balance and deliciousness. It feels great going down. It's a true staple, and I've explored a long list of variations on the theme since then.

MAKES ⅓ CUP

2½ teaspoons dried turmeric

⅓ cup | 80 ml good, raw honey

1 lemon

Lots of freshly ground black pepper

Drizzle of pure almond oil or coconut milk, or ½ teaspoon extra-virgin coconut oil or ghee (page 314)

Work the turmeric into the honey until it forms a paste. You can keep this on hand, in a jar, for whenever you'd like a cup without much fuss. It will keep stored in a dark cupboard nearly indefinitely.

For each cup, place a heaping teaspoon of the turmeric paste in the bottom of a mug. Pour hot (but not boiling) water into the mug and stir well to dissolve the turmeric paste. Add a big squeeze of juice from the lemon, a good amount of black pepper, and a finishing drizzle of almond oil, or coconut milk, extra-virgin coconut oil or ghee. Stir now and then as you drink so all the good stuff doesn't settle to the bottom, or top off with more hot water as you drink it.

Variations: Lime juice in place of lemon juice; a bit of grated raw ginger or fresh ginger juice (page 316); hot almond milk in place of water.

Ruby Ginger Juice

orange ∗ grapefruit ∗ fresh ginger

My winter elixir—a sunset-shaded jolt of ginger-spiked citrus. Strong, invigorating, and bright, seen here with a blend of Cara Cara oranges, Ruby Red grapefruit, and lemon. There are infinite variations on the general idea. Experiment with the best of the season's citrus and serve strong and cold in a tiny glass. For a boozy brunch, add a bottle of rosé or sparkling rosé to the whole batch.

SERVES 4

2 tablespoons natural cane sugar or honey

1 cup | 240 ml water

2 tablespoons grated fresh ginger

1 Cara Cara orange

2 Ruby Red grapefruits

1 lemon

In a small saucepan, combine the sugar, water, and ginger. Bring to a simmer, remove from heat, and let sit for a few minutes while you juice the citrus into a separate bowl. You can either strain the citrus juice or leave it pulpy. Strain the ginger water into a small pitcher, stir in the citrus juice mixture, and taste, adjusting with more sweetener as you like. Serve cold.

Variations: Use the juice of 2 Ruby Red grapefruits, 3 Page mandarins, and 1 lemon; use the juice of 2 limes and 2 cocktail grapefruits; make into a slushy by mixing in a blender with ample ice.

Pimm's Cup

green coriander seeds * cucumber * ginger beer

I had my first real sampling of Pimm's cups while in London during an uncharacteristic heat wave—kids and adults played in Hyde Park fountains late into the afternoons, and every pub offered its own house-blended Pimm's cup cooler. Served in ice-filled glasses, the refreshing, citrus herbaceousness of Pimm's goes down easy. It's a top-flight warm-weather quencher on the handful of days each year when the fog clears and temperatures shoot up in San Francisco.

Look for Classic No. 1 Pimm's: it's gin-based, with citrus notes that compliment the fresh coriander seeds that are often abundant in gardens and markets in late spring and throughout summer.

SERVES 2

1 (1-inch | 2.5cm) segment of cucumber, thinly sliced

1 teaspoon fresh green coriander seeds

1 cup | 240 ml Pimm's

2 tablespoons freshly squeezed lemon juice

½ cup | 120 ml strong ginger beer

Delicately sliced cucumbers, plums, lemons, seasonal fruit, and/or fresh coriander sprigs, for garnish

Muddle the cucumber and coriander seeds with a pestle in a cocktail glass or wide-mouth mason jar. Add the Pimm's and lemon juice and a handful of ice cubes. Cover and shake vigorously. Chill two glasses and fill with ice. Strain the cocktail mixture into the glasses, top off with ginger beer, and finish with cucumbers or fruit, and sprigs of fresh coriander.

NOTE: If you don't have fresh coriander seeds, smash a small bundle of cilantro leaves and stems in their place. You can use a proper cocktail muddler or a pestle, or in a pinch, a wooden spoon—the idea is to crush and press the ingredients into a flavor-saturated base of refreshing deliciousness.

En Route

OTHER IMMUNIZATIONS/PROPHYLAXIS RECEIVED
Autres vaccinations/prophylaxies reçues

This space is provided to record immunizations/prophylaxis that are not required for entrance into any country but
have been obtained by the traveler for additional health protection (immune globulin, malaria, measles, etc.)

Date	Vaccine/prophylactic drug Vaccin/médicament prophylactique	Dose	Physician's signature Signature du médecin
NOV 1 7 1999	DIPT/TET.	0.5cc.	OVERSEAS MEDICAL CENTER 49 Drumm Street
NOV 1 7 1999	POLIO INJECTION	0.5cc	San Francisco, Calif. 94111
NOV 1 7 1999	MENINGITIS	0.5cc.	OVERSEAS MEDICAL CENTER 49 Drumm Street San Francisco, Calif. 94111
JAN 1 2 2000	HAVRIX		
JAN 1 2 2000	CHOLERA	0.5cc	OVERSEAS MEDICAL CENTER
JAN 1 2 2000	TYPHOID	0.5cc	49 Drumm Street
FEB 0 9 2004	Typhim V	0.5	San Francisco, CALIF. 94111 49 Drumm Street
FEB 0 9 2004	Hep A#1	.14	San Francisco, Calif. 94111
AUG 0 9 2012	Tdap.	0.5cc	CPMC TRAVEL CLINIC 3801 SACRAMENTO ST. S.F. CA 94118
AUG 0 9 2012	Typhim V	0.5cc	CPMC TRAVEL CLINIC 3801 SACRAMENTO ST. S.F. CA 94118
AUG 0 9 2012	Hep B#1	1 cc.	CPMC TRAVEL CLINIC 3801 SACRAMENTO ST.
SEP 2 0 2012	Hep B #2	1 cc.	S.F. CA 94118
Feb 08 2013	Hep B #3	1 cc.	S.F. CA 94118

A FLIP THROUGH THE PASSPORT in my office drawer reveals stamps from Chile, Tanzania, France, Sri Lanka, Czech Republic, Italy, Thailand, Netherlands, Spain, Morocco, India, Japan, Argentina, Mexico, and England. A few times a year I leave my day-to-day routine behind to hop planes, buses, trains, and ferries, snapping photos, eating in new places, and chatting with people on subway platforms and in cafés. I try to turn down streets I've never explored before, shop at unfamiliar markets, and cook in kitchens not my own.

Correspondingly, there have been plenty of hot, dusty bus rides, sketchy flights, vaccinations, and botched conversations in my past. Travel isn't always easy or comfortable. It's rarely perfect or glamorous—but because I dragged an overstuffed duffel bag through the dirt streets and alleys of Dar es Salaam before sunrise one morning, I was sitting on the roof of an old hotel in Zanzibar by evening, with the sun smearing out over the horizon in a hazy-hot orange. The air smelled of ylang-ylang, and the call to prayer reverberated off the metal roofs of Stone Town. Sometimes, after I've returned home, I think of the horns in New Delhi—an ongoing symphony of honking vehicles, the staccato beeps of the tiny cars punctuated by the occasional bassoon of the big lorries. I remember the sansho and cayenne in the air of the tiny shop in Kyoto where a friendly man blended vibrant shichimi togarashi to order. And the red dragonflies in Chiang Mai, so different from the dragonflies at the park near my home in San Francisco, which flash green.

A big part of any trip is getting there, getting around, and getting home. It often involves long flights, delayed trains, and unpredictability. It's important to feel good and strong when traveling. So I'm religious about packing nutritious portables for each journey.

Chive Dumplings

green split peas ✳ spinach ✳ coconut milk

I bring these on the longest of flights, and I'm never sorry I made the extra effort to cook them up in the mad scramble to get out the door. Aside from being travel-friendly, they can be a quick afternoon snack, great finger food for a party, or the basis of a meal (alongside a big salad) for dinner. I use green split peas here, but you can swap green lentils or mung beans if you like. You can also steam these or poach them in a thin broth.

MAKES ABOUT 2 DOZEN
DUMPLINGS

CHIVE OIL

½ cup | 120 ml
    sunflower oil

½ cup | 1 oz | 30 g finely
    chopped chives

Fine-grain sea salt

---

2 cups | 11 oz | 310 g cooked
    green split peas, at room
    temperature

½ to ¾ cup | 120 to
    180 ml coconut milk
    or half-and-half

½ teaspoon fine-grain
    sea salt

1 medium garlic clove,
    smashed to a paste

1 cup well-packed | 1.5 oz
    | 40 g spinach

⅓ cup | 0.75 oz | 20 g
    chopped chives

1 package 4-inch | 10cm
    round pot sticker
    wrappers

1 tablespoon sunflower oil,
    or as needed

To make the chive oil, use a food processor to puree the oil with half of the chives. Stir in the remaining chives by hand and season with a couple of pinches of salt. Set aside. Note: You can refrigerate this for later use, but bring to room temperature before using.

Pulse the split peas in a food processor until uniform and fluffy. Add ½ cup | 120 ml of the coconut milk, the salt, and garlic and pulse until uniform and smooth. Pulse in the spinach and chives, then more coconut milk, a tablespoon at a time, until the mixture is the consistency of extra-tacky Play-Doh. Taste and add more salt if needed.

To fill and shape the dumplings, very lightly dust your counter with flour. Place 12 wrappers on the floured countertop, add a small dollop of filling just off center of each dumpling and run a wet finger around the rim of the wrappers. Press the edges together well and try to avoid trapping air bubbles in the dumplings if you can. Crimp each dumpling and gently press it down against the counter to give it a flat base, so it sits upright. This base is also what gets brown and crunchy—one of the things you're after. Repeat until you run out of wrappers or fill-ing. Place the dumplings seam side up on a well-floured plate or baking sheet. The extra flour that sticks to the base gives extra crunch. At this point you can freeze any dump-lings you know you aren't going to cook.

To cook the dumplings, heat the sunflower oil in a large skillet over medium-high heat. Arrange the dumplings in the pan, seam side up, with a sliver of space between each (so they don't stick together—cook in batches if neces-sary). Pan-fry until the bottoms are golden, a few minutes. With a lid that will cover the skillet in one hand, carefully and quickly add ⅓ cup | 80 ml of water to the pan, imme-diately cover, and cook the dumplings for a few minutes, until the water is nearly evaporated. Uncover and finish cooking until all the water is gone, another minute or so. Dial back the heat if the bottoms are getting too dark. Repeat with remaining dumplings, adding more oil to the pan, if needed.

Serve drizzled with the chive oil.

Spring Rolls

ginger onion paste ✳ brown sugar tofu ✳ mushrooms

At a glance, this recipe looks a bit component-y, but that's just the nature of spring rolls. They actually come together pretty quickly, and the good news is you can prep the onion paste and tofu a day or two ahead of time. Here's how these work. Each roll has a slather of ginger onion paste, a couple of crunchy lettuce leaves, some mushrooms, some tofu, and a bit of cilantro (or other herb of your choice—mint, basil). Roll tight, and you're set. They're one of my favorite things to bring along on long flights—filled with fresh, healthy ingredients and quite resilient. The sort of meal that makes eating in transit something to look forward to.

MAKES 1 DOZEN
SPRING ROLLS

About 1 dozen rice paper wrappers

½ cup | 120 ml Ginger Onion Paste (page 109)

1 head crisp, crunchy lettuce, either Baby Gem or romaine

Brown Sugar Tofu & Mushrooms (page 108)

1 small bunch cilantro or other fresh herbs

To assemble, dip a rice paper wrapper into a bowl of hot water for just 3 seconds. Resist oversoaking—even if the paper is a bit stiff, it will continue to absorb water as you assemble the wrap. Place on a flat work surface and fold in half. (Have a glance at the photo if you've never done this.) You're going to want to keep all of your ingredients crowded into one-third of the available surface of the wrapper at this point. First, put down a generous smear of ginger onion paste. Add a lettuce leaf or two, a little tofu, a few mushrooms, and some cilantro, then tuck the wrapper over the filling and roll it up. I like open-sided rolls, but you can certainly make enclosed rolls by leaving the wrapper round and folding in the edges mid-wrap.

Brown Sugar Tofu & Mushrooms

garlic * sunflower oil

By coating tofu and mushrooms with a bit of brown sugar, you get a nice amount of caramelization where the ingredients touch the pan. I mainly make this as a filling for the Spring Rolls (page 106), but it makes for a quick side as well—you can add a bit of chopped kale in order to work in some greens and make it a true one-pan meal. My mushroom of choice here is nameko— amber in color, with an earthy, butterscotch flavor. But enoki and regular brown mushrooms are A-plus as well.

SERVES 4, OR MAKES FILLING
FOR A DOZEN SPRING ROLLS
(PAGE 106)

12 oz | 340 g extra-firm tofu

3 medium cloves garlic

½ teaspoon fine-grain sea salt

4 teaspoons natural brown sugar

2 tablespoons sunflower oil, plus more if needed

8 oz | 225 g mushrooms, brushed clean, sliced ¼ inch | 6 mm thick

Pat the tofu dry and cut into 6 equal slabs before arranging in a single layer on a rimmed plate. Place the garlic in a mortar and pestle, sprinkle with the salt and sugar, and pound into a paste. Work the oil in a bit at a time, continuing to work the ingredients until they come together. Scrape the paste onto the tofu slices and use your hands to gently slather and coat each piece of tofu with the paste; be quite thorough. Place the tofu in a single layer in a large skillet over medium-high heat and cook until deeply golden on each side, 5 minutes or so. It's likely you won't need any additional oil here; if you do, add to the pan a small splash at a time. Remove the tofu from the pan, and when cool enough to handle, slice into pencil-thick pieces and sprinkle with salt to taste.

While the tofu is cooking, toss the mushrooms gently (but well) in the residual marinade left in the plate that held the tofu. Once the tofu is done, use the same skillet to cook the mushrooms over high heat, stirring just a couple of times along the way, until the mushrooms release and evaporate their water and take on a nice, dark color. Transfer to a bowl or platter and season with a bit more salt if needed. Keep the tofu and mushrooms separate if you plan to use them in the spring rolls or toss and serve together as an easy side.

Ginger Onion Paste

sunflower oil ✳ shallots ✳ sea salt

This paste is regularly used to deliver a punch of flavor to my Spring Rolls (page 106), but you can use it in many other ways as well. I use it to cook scrambled eggs; I cook soba noodles, drain them, and toss them with a few spoonfuls of this; and I drizzle it over just-cooked (or grilled) vegetables. You can make this paste with few pulses in a food processor, but I prefer the texture you can achieve with the mortar and pestle.

MAKES ABOUT
½ CUP | 120 ML

2 green onions, finely sliced

3 medium shallots, finely sliced

3 tablespoons peeled grated ginger

Scant ½ teaspoon fine-grain sea salt

6 tablespoons | 90 ml unrefined sunflower oil

Place the onions, shallots, and ginger in a mortar and sprinkle with the salt. Pound with the pestle until the onions are quite bruised, but not pastelike. Heat the oil in a small saucepan until hot enough that you could sauté something in it. Add the onion mixture to the oil, remove from the heat, and transfer to a jar to cool. I like to drain off (and save) most of the oil before using it in the spring rolls, leaving just the paste.

Strong Ginger Snaps

honey * ground ginger * unsulfured molasses

I'm one of those people who need to follow some rules when it comes to long flights. This means drink a lot of water, pass on alcohol, pack my own food, and get a good night's sleep the night before. Still, if a flight is more than ten or eleven hours long, I tend to get headachy and queasy, and I've found a jolt of ginger really helps. I now pack a little bag of these tiny, intense ginger boosts for the tail end of long-haul journeys. This is the straightforward version, but I also love to make them with a few handfuls of chopped, toasted hazelnuts or pecans added to the dough along with the flour.

MAKES 4 TO 5 DOZEN
SMALL COOKIES

1 cup | 8 oz | 225 g unsalted butter, at room temperature

¾ cup | 5.5 oz | 160 g granulated sugar

3½ cups | 1 lb | 450 g whole wheat pastry flour

5 tablespoons | 0.625 oz | 20 g ground ginger

1½ tablespoons baking soda

2½ teaspoons non-aluminum baking powder

Scant 1 teaspoon fine-grain sea salt

1 cup runny honey, at room temperature

2 tablespoons good-tasting, unsulfured molasses

Preheat the oven to 350°F | 175°C. Line two baking sheets with parchment paper.

Beat the butter with an electric mixer until light and fluffy. Add the sugar and continue to mix until billowy and light. Combine the flour, ginger, baking soda, baking powder, and salt in a bowl, then mix into the butter mixture in two additions, mixing just enough to produce a crumbly texture. Add the honey and molasses and mix just long enough for the dough to come together cohesively.

Use your hands to fashion tiny ¾-inch | 2cm balls of dough and arrange, well apart, on the prepared baking sheets (if you are baking all the cookies at once, you'll need to work in batches). Bake for 10 to 12 minutes, or until the bottoms are nicely golden. Remove from the oven, let sit for a couple of minutes, and transfer the cookies to a cooling rack. Bake the remaining cookies or freeze the dough balls for later use. When baking from frozen, extend the oven time just a bit.

Far

MOROCCO

Marrakech * *Essaouira* * *Fes*

THE SLIVER OF MOROCCO I'VE SEEN is an invigorating collision of old and new, ancient and modern—ingredients, apothecary, customs, architecture, and infrastructure. Get an early enough start and you can watch the markets in the medinas come to life. Metal hand cranks squeak as merchants lower their canvas awnings and then retract their metal security doors. In the center of the souk umbrellas bloom in sun-bleached patterns—pastel paisleys, botanicals, gingham, polka dots, pencil-thin stripes of pink interlacing turquoise, oversized white leaves on bright kelly green. Quince is sold next to purslane; carts of pomegranate, prickly pears, apples, and garlic are displayed alongside rubber tires. Canary melons are piled next to boy's briefs. Men play checkers with bottle caps—plastic versus metal.

The ancient medinas are tricky and sometimes bewildering to the uninitiated—but not for long. You learn. To find the way back to my *riad* in Marrakech, I knew to walk west from Jemaa el-Fna square one hundred paces before turning north past a satellite receiver store and the sunglasses stand. Then pass the cell phone vendor and the café where the workers on the block take their coffee. Turn right through Bab el Ksour, and right again into an alley punctuated by a single brass lantern paned with colored glass. From my base here it was easy to explore the souks of the old city.

One side of our room was made up by a thick stretch of the medina wall—the sort of dense material that is always cold when you put your cheek to it, despite the heat outdoors. I'd pull the old cedar shutters

115

open in the morning and watch the locals go about their morning routine. There was one woman in particular I'd wait for. She would arrive at a *bessara* soup stall just across the way and begin working small balls of dough—pressing, folding, pressing, folding. I'd run down just as the first *msemmen* flatbreads were coming off her griddle.

My Moroccan Pantry

ALMONDS

ARGAN OIL

BARLEY

BUTTERMILK

CHICKPEAS

CHILES

CILANTRO

CINNAMON

CITRUS

COUSCOUS

CORIANDER

CUCUMBER

CUMIN

DATES

DRIED FRUIT

DRIED GINGER

EGGS

FRESH HERBS

HONEY

LEMON VERBENA

LENTILS

MINT

OLIVES

ORANGE BLOSSOM WATER

POMEGRANATES

POMEGRANATE SYRUP

PRESERVED LEMON

PRICKLY PEARS

RAS EL HANOUT

ROSE WATER AND DRIED PETALS

SAFFRON

SAGE

TOMATOES

TURMERIC

YOGURT

Beghrir

semolina flour * yeast * toasted sesame

The busiest thoroughfares in the Fes medina are lined with vendors—food and otherwise. The slight man on the corner with a foot-high stack of beghrir was the one who got my daily business. He sold massive, yeasted semolina breakfast crumpets with inch-thick stalactite honeycombing. Each piece a golden marvel, cut to order, offered drizzled with honey or slathered with farm cheese, wrapped in paper. Not quite as dramatic, these are a compelling version, simple to make on any griddle or skillet.

SERVES 4

½ cup | 120 ml warm water (110°F to 115°F | 43°C to 46°C)

½ teaspoon runny honey

2 teaspoons | 7 g active dry yeast (one packet)

1½ cups | 9 oz | 255 g fine semolina flour

2 cups | 9 oz | 255 g all-purpose flour

1 teaspoon fine-grain sea salt

2 tablespoons toasted sesame seeds (optional)

2 eggs

⅔ cup | 160 ml milk

1¾ cups | 415 ml water

Butter, for frying and serving

Saffron Honey (facing page), to serve

Place the warm water in a small bowl and stir in the honey. Sprinkle the yeast over the top, stir well, and set aside until the yeast blooms on the surface, 10 minutes or so. In the meantime, whisk together the flours, salt, and sesame seeds in a large bowl. In a separate bowl, whisk the eggs with the milk and water. Pour this mixture over the flours, add the yeast liquid, and use a hand blender to combine until the batter is smooth and light. Cover with a towel and place in a warm spot for an hour.

When you're ready to cook the *beghrir*, melt a teaspoon of butter in a large skillet or saucepan over medium heat. Ladle roughly 3 tablespoons of batter into the pan and smooth with the back of the ladle into a small circle. Repeat this process until your pan is full. Cook on one side until the surface erupts in tiny holes, the bottom is golden, and the top has erupted in tiny holes and set. Remove from the pan and repeat with the remaining batter. These are best served immediately off the griddle, but you can keep finished pancakes warm by wrapping them in a clean dishtowel on a plate. Serve topped with more butter and saffron honey.

Saffron Honey

wildflower honey ✳ vanilla extract ✳ saffron

The night before I left
for my first visit to Morocco,
my friend Naya hosted
a Morocco-inspired feast
where, among an impressive
spread of salads, couscous,
and tagines, she served a
saffron honey she'd picked
up on her own travels. It
was vibrant yellow and
had intense saffron flavor.
Drizzled over goat cheese
as a start to the meal, it
was a revelation. After some
consideration, I eventually
thought of a good way to
replicate that honey. Saffron
is not only water soluble,
but also alcohol soluble, so
I began by soaking saffron
threads in a small splash of
vanilla or almond extract
before whisking it into
honey for an immediate,
intense infusion.

MAKES ½ CUP
| 120 ML HONEY

2 pinches of saffron (about
40 threads)

1 teaspoon vanilla extract
or almond extract

½ cup | 120 ml runny
wildflower honey

Place the saffron threads in a tiny bowl. Add the extract and stir until the saffron is wet. Let sit for 10 minutes before stirring the saffron mixture into the honey. You'll want to stir well, until the honey is uniform and the threads are evenly distributed throughout. The honey can be stored indefinitely in a glass jar in a dark pantry.

NOTE: Saffron honey is wonderful over soft tangy cheese and yogurt and also over yeasted Beghrir (facing page)—the honey melds with butter on the warm cakes and drops down into the honeycomb pockets. Few things are better.

Fresh Tomato Salad

cumin ✳ cilantro ✳ red spring onions

A Berber apothecary is a wonder. You'll come across these pharmacies—an expression of the indigenous Berber people—in medinas and elsewhere around Morocco: shelves lined with bottles, baskets filled with roots, planks piled with fragrant spices. The line between cooking and wellness and medicine here is wonderfully intact. Cumin is always prominent—used whole or ground as a remedy for a long list of ailments, it also appears ubiquitously at the Moroccan table as a condiment.

Use your best, in-season cherry tomatoes for this. A smear of goat cheese on a tear of Moroccan bread with a bit of this folded in is a fine thing. And I like to sprinkle a few cilantro sprigs and fresh coriander seeds across the top here when in season—which is typically about the time tomatoes are starting to look good.

SERVES 4

¾ teaspoon cumin seeds

1 cup | 4.5 oz | 125 g finely chopped red spring onion

1 basket cherry tomatoes, stemmed

4 zucchini blossoms, cut into chiffonade

Flaky sea salt

½ cup | 0.5 oz | 15 g chopped cilantro leaves and stems

2 to 3 tablespoons extra-virgin olive oil

Fresh coriander seeds or chopped cilantro, to serve

In a dry skillet over medium heat, toast the cumin until fragrant. Transfer to a mortar and pestle and smash a bit. Set aside. Place the onions in a small bowl and cover with ice water to mellow its bite a little. Set aside while you prep the rest of the ingredients.

Slice each tomato in two or three and arrange along with most of the zucchini flowers on a platter. Sprinkle a bit of salt across the top, and then the cumin, seasoning the tomatoes. Drain the onions well, pat dry, and toss with the cilantro. Arrange this mixture atop the tomatoes, drizzle generously with the olive oil, and finish with a few fresh coriander seeds and the remaining zucchini blossoms.

Chicory Soup

barley ✳ preserved lemon relish ✳ ancho chile

Preserved lemons are the chewy, salty, puckery gems of the Moroccan table. And while you can make your own, they're increasingly easy to come by in many stores. I've tried to thread different ways to use them throughout this chapter, so you don't end up buying a jar for one recipe and letting the rest go to waste. They're bright bursts in simple salads, vinaigrettes, or in a chile relish like the one I make here to top a hearty, unfussy barley soup. You can use the chopped peel, or the entire lemon (seeded).

You'll find assorted types of chicories in the winter and fall; they're related to lettuce, but more bitter, and generally more structured. For this soup a blend of Castelfranco radicchio and escarole works nicely, but you can select just one. I also like to use a bit of the barley cooking water in place of some of the water called for here.

SERVES 4

7 tablespoons | 105 ml extra-virgin olive oil, plus more for serving

1 medium onion, quartered and thinly sliced

2 cups | 8 oz | 225 g diced celery

Fine-grain sea salt

1 bay leaf

3 sprigs fresh thyme

7 cups | 1.65 L water

3 cups | 15 oz | 425 g cooked barley

1 large dried ancho chile

1 large clove garlic, smashed

1 small whole preserved lemon, rinsed, seeded, and minced

3 cups | 4 oz | 115 g chicory, cut into 1½-inch | 4cm pieces

Crème fraîche, chopped cilantro, and/or chopped chives, to serve

To a large pot over medium heat, add 3 tablespoons of the olive oil, the onion, celery, and 2½ teaspoons of salt. Stir frequently for 5 to 10 minutes, until the onions and celery are soft but not browned. Add the bay, thyme, and water and let simmer for about 20 minutes, until the vegetables are very tender. Stir in the cooked barley. Continue to simmer for an additional 10 to 20 minutes, until the starchy barley has slightly thickened the broth. Remove and discard the bay leaf and thyme sprigs. Taste again for seasoning, adjusting if necessary.

While the soup is simmering, make a lemon-chile relish. Start by removing the stem, ribs, and seeds from the chile. Chop the chile into very small, irregular crumbles. You want bits that are not uniform, to lend a rustic quality to the final result. In a small pot over medium heat, combine the remaining 4 tablespoons of olive oil, the chile crumbles, and garlic. Tilt the pan so that the oil pools, toasting the chile, but taking care not to burn the garlic. After about 5 minutes the chile should be somewhat softened and its flavor will have infused the oil. Remove the

pan from the heat, smash up the garlic pieces, and stir in the preserved lemon.

To serve, toss the chicory with a small splash of olive oil and a sprinkling of salt. Ladle soup into individual bowls then top with the dressed chicory. Add small spoonfuls of lemon-ancho relish, dabs of crème fraîche, and lots of chopped cilantro and chives.

Grated Cucumber Salad

oregano * olives * almonds

From the sky departing Fes-Saïss Airport, olive trees dot the camel-colored hills of northern Morocco like intricate embroidery patterns. Not surprisingly, you see their fruit appear in many guises on the Moroccan table—punctuating simple salads like this one, nestled in tagines, and easing up aside citrus. You'll want to use European cucumbers if you can find them—they're smaller with more assertive flavor. And please opt for a box grater and not a Microplane for grating here.

SERVES 4 TO 6

1 medium clove garlic

¼ teaspoon fine-grain sea salt

20 fresh oregano leaves

⅓ cup | 1 oz | 30 g toasted sliced almonds

3 medium cucumbers, seeded and grated

1½ tablespoons freshly squeezed lemon juice

1 teaspoon honey

15 black olives, pitted, rinsed, and chopped

1 tablespoon minced preserved lemon rind

2 tablespoons extra-virgin olive oil

Place the garlic in a mortar, sprinkle with the salt, and use the pestle to grind into a paste. Add the oregano and work it into an herby mess. Add the almonds and smash into a rough sandy texture—don't go too far, or you'll end up with almond butter. Use your fingers to lighten it up a bit. Set aside until you're ready to serve.

Wrap the grated cucumber in a clean kitchen towel (or paper towels) and really press to remove moisture. Aim to get it as dry as you can without destroying the cucumber. Transfer to a bowl and fluff with your fingertips. Toss well with lemon juice and honey. Add the olives and most of the minced preserved lemon and toss again. Just before serving, sprinkle with the almond mixture and the remaining preserved lemon and drizzle with olive oil.

Saffron Tagine

chickpeas ✳ yellow wax beans ✳
saffron ✳ *ras el hanout*

One afternoon, while browsing a naturopathy store in Marrakech's newer Euro-modern district, Gueliz, also known as Ville Nouvelle, I came across a stack of little pots of unusually fragrant saffron. I asked the shopkeeper about it and he proudly informed me this saffron was from the most recent harvest in Taliouine, a place where the Crocus sativus flower blooms in the midst of olive branches, wild herbs, and almonds trees. I brought a purse of the saffron home with me and now reserve it for this, my favorite tagine, where it plays perfectly among silky, tender slow-cooked vegetables.

In early summer I use fresh chickpeas, leeks, potatoes, and whatever looks beautiful here. But you can adapt the recipe as the seasons change. For those of you without a tagine, any thick pot or casserole will do.

SERVES 4

Pinch of saffron (about 20 threads)

2 teaspoons ras el hanout

1¼ teaspoons fine-grain sea salt

¼ cup | 2 oz | 60 g clarified butter (see page 315)

3 cloves garlic, sliced paper-thin

1 pound | 455 g small, waxy potatoes, sliced ¾ inch | 2 cm thick

3 medium leeks, trimmed, washed, and sliced

3 cups | 710 ml water or vegetable stock

4 spring onions, or 8 green onions, trimmed and halved

4 oz | 115 g yellow wax beans, ends trimmed

⅔ cup | 4 oz | 115 g fresh or cooked chickpeas

2 to 4 eggs (optional)

4 dates or prunes, chopped

Toasted sesame seeds, lemon wedges, fresh basil, and/or argan oil, to serve

Grind the saffron, *ras el hanout*, and salt together in a mortar and pestle until powder fine.

In an 11-inch | 28cm tagine or large casserole over medium heat, melt the clarified butter and add the garlic, potatoes, and leeks. Stir to coat, cook until the leeks soften, then sprinkle with the saffron spice salt. Arrange everything in a shallow, even layer and add enough water to barely cover most of the potatoes. Arrange the spring onions in a cluster, bring everything to a simmer, dial back the heat, cover, and cook until the potatoes are tender, 20 to 25 minutes.

About 10 minutes before the potatoes finish cooking, nest the wax beans and chickpeas in the tagine; a few minutes after that, carefully crack however many eggs you'd like near the outer rim. Cover and cook until the egg yolks are cooked to your liking.

To serve, arrange an egg in each bowl, with vegetables to the side, spoon the broth over the top, and serve with a cluster of dates. A squeeze of lemon and drizzle of argan oil is a nice addition, as are sesame seeds and fresh basil.

Harira

chickpeas ✴ lentils ✴ cilantro ✴ warm spices

Hearty, filling, and beautifully fragrant, this is a spice-forward vegetarian version of harira, *the traditional soup eaten to break the fast each day during the month of Ramadan—it's also a staple on many menus throughout Morocco. There's a long list of ingredients here, but don't let that dissuade—you likely have many of them on hand. I like to introduce cilantro leaves and stems at multiple points in the cooking process for the best flavor. Also, seek out* lentilles du Puy *or black lentils here (or use a blend of the two); these varietals keep their shape best throughout the cooking process.*

SERVES 6 TO 8

1 bunch cilantro

½ cup | 120 ml extra-virgin olive oil

2 medium onions, diced

3 celery stalks, diced, leaves reserved

6 cloves garlic, very thinly sliced

2 tablespoons minced fresh ginger

Pinch of saffron (about 30 threads)

2½ teaspoons fine-grain sea salt

½ teaspoon ground cinnamon

2½ teaspoons sweet paprika

½ teaspoon crushed red pepper flakes

2½ teaspoons ground cumin

2 cups | 10 oz | 280 g cooked chickpeas

1½ cups | 9 oz | 255 g dried lentils, picked over and rinsed

6 cups | 1.5 L water

4 to 5 tablespoons all-purpose flour (see Note, page 140)

Scant ¼ cup | 50 ml freshly squeezed lemon juice

1 (28-oz | 795g) can whole tomatoes

2 tablespoons chopped fresh marjoram or oregano

3 oz | 55 g angel hair pasta, broken into 1-inch | 2.5cm pieces (see Note, page 140)

Chopped fresh dates, to serve

Chop the cilantro stems finely and set aside in a pile. Chop the leaves and reserve separately. Heat ⅓ cup | 80 ml of the olive oil in a large soup pot over medium-high heat. Add the onions, celery, garlic, ginger, and cilantro stems, stir to coat, and cook until everything softens a bit, 5 minutes or so. Grind the saffron with the salt into a powder with a mortar and pestle and add to the pot along with the cinnamon, sweet paprika, red pepper flakes, and cumin. Stir well before adding the chickpeas and lentils. Stir in 4 cups | 1 L of the water and bring to a simmer.

In a separate large bowl, gradually whisk the remaining 2 cups | 500 ml of water into the flour, a splash at a time to avoid lumps. Add the lemon juice, tomatoes with their juice, and most of the remaining cilantro. Stir well,

breaking up the tomatoes somewhat. Add this mixture to the soup and bring to a simmer, stirring often. Once at a simmer, cook for another 15 to 20 minutes, stirring occasionally, until the lentils are cooked through. When you have about 5 minutes left, stir in the marjoram and pasta. Once the pasta is cooked, adjust the seasoning and serve topped with dates, the remaining cilantro, the remaining olive oil, and the reserved celery leaves.

NOTE: For a gluten-free version, substitute 2 to 3 tablespoons of cornstarch for the all-purpose flour, and omit the pasta.

Dried Fruit Salad

apricots ✳ avocado ✳ parsley ✳ preserved lemon

Dried fruit is everywhere in Moroccan markets—apricots, dates, grapes, and figs stacked in rows or gummy grids. You see them in carts, on shelves, piled atop baskets, and displayed on wide shallow platters. Vendors swat with plastic horsetails to keep the flies at bay. This is a simple dried fruit salad to serve as a side dish or as part of an assembly of salads.

It is also traditional to serve a bit of chopped date in Harira (page 138)—this would be a nice alternative. If you can find unsulfured fruit, use it.

SERVES 4

1 cup | 5 oz | 140 g halved dried apricots

1 cup | 5 oz | 140 g pitted and quartered dried Medjool dates

¼ cup | 60 ml extra-virgin olive oil

¼ teaspoon fine-grain sea salt

1 teaspoon minced preserved lemon

¾ cup | 0.75 oz | 20 g parsley leaves

1 medium avocado, cubed

In a bowl, combine the apricots, dates, olive oil, salt, preserved lemon, and parsley. Toss well. Add the avocado and do a last gentle toss. Adjust the seasoning and serve at room temperature.

Ginger Orange Blossom Water

ginger juice ✶ pomegranate ✶ orange blossom water

I took my last trip to Morocco in November, in large part because I'd read an essay in The Atlantic *by Curtis Cate. It was penned in 1961 and starts with him saying, "Morocco is a land which should be visited in winter. It is in November, when elsewhere in the Northern Hemisphere the yellow-brown leaves have fallen and the plants have tucked themselves into their beds of cold earth, that the flowers of Morocco come to life. The walls don capes of crimson and purple bougainvillea, the gardens spill over with red-blossomed hibiscus, pink laurel, green myrtle, and lily-white arum, while the air grows heavy with the fragrance of jasmine, orange blossoms, and trumpet lilies."*

In the souks you'll see shelves lined with recycled glass bottles and jugs of various blossom waters—often hand-labeled: orange blossom, rose blossom, chamomile blossom. They can be used to accent any number of baked goods, salads, or beverages. One thing to keep in mind: Some blossom waters are stronger than others. Always start with a small splash.

SERVES 4

1 tablespoon fresh ginger juice (page 316)

1 tablespoon pomegranate syrup

1 cup | 240 ml sparkling water

½ cup | 120 ml freshly squeezed grapefruit juice

2 to 3 teaspoons orange blossom water

Fill a cocktail shaker half full with ice cubes. Add the ginger juice, pomegranate syrup, sparkling water, grapefruit juice, and 2 teaspoons of the orange blossom water. Cover and shake vigorously. Add more orange blossom water ½ teaspoon at a time to your liking. Shake one last time. Fill four glasses with ice and evenly divide the mixture among them. Top off with more sparkling water if you like.

Herb Jam

various greens ✳ *oily black olives* ✳ *smoked paprika*

Paula Wolfert had me daydreaming of the souks and sights of Morocco long before I set foot there. This is a lazy variation of the herb jam Paula includes in a number of her books. A massive bundle of spinach, parsley, and celery leaves cook down to a compact jar of dark, heady jam primed to be slathered on everything from flatbread to focaccia. Stir it into eggs, pasta, couscous, and bowls of whatever grains you have on hand. Paula emphatically tells you to steam the greens (not sauté), but my steamer struggles with the amount of spinach required. Instead, I cook the greens down in a large pot, just long enough that they're tender and easily choppable. Texturally it's a different beast than Paula's, but moreish just the same.

MAKES 2½ CUPS | 590 ML

4 tablespoons | 60 ml extra-virgin olive oil, plus more if needed

4 large garlic cloves, smashed

12 oil-cured black olives, pitted, rinsed, and chopped

1¼ teaspoons smoked paprika

¼ teaspoon cayenne

⅛ teaspoon ground cumin

1 pound | 455 g baby spinach leaves

1 bunch flat-leaf parsley, stems removed (about 2 cups | 2 oz | 55 g)

½ cup | 0.5 oz | 15 g chopped fresh celery leaves

½ cup | 0.5 oz | 15 g cilantro leaves and stems

Freshly squeezed lemon juice

½ teaspoon fine-grain sea salt

In your largest pot combine 2 tablespoons of the olive oil and the garlic over medium-low heat. Cook gently until it has softened but not browned, 5 minutes or so. Stir in the olives, paprika, cayenne, and ground cumin and stir for a minute or so, until fragrant. Turn up the heat to medium-high and immediately stir in the spinach, parsley, celery leaves, and cilantro, stirring constantly, until everything collapses into a bright tangle. Cook until the greens release their liquid, then allow it to cook off a bit—all told, 2 to 3 minutes. Remove from heat and carefully transfer the greens to a cutting board. Let cool a few minutes, then chop finely.

Transfer to a jar, stir in a bit of lemon juice, the salt, and the remaining 2 tablespoons olive oil. The herb jam will keep, covered, in the refrigerator for a few days. Serve, preferably at room temperature.

Roasted Tomato Salad

heirloom tomatoes ✴ harissa oil ✴
strained yogurt ✴ lettuce

*The next time you think
of making a caprese salad,
consider this instead.
A bright harissa oil
brings an element of the
unexpected to this toss-up
of summer's best raw and
roasted tomatoes. You can
roast the tomatoes and
prepare the harissa oil
ahead of time. Keep the
roasted tomatoes in a jar
covered in oil, bring to room
temperature, and drain
before continuing with
the recipe.*

SERVES 4 TO 6

2 pounds | 900 g
    tomatoes (a mix of
    small heirlooms and
    cherry tomatoes),
    halved

2 tablespoons plus ⅓ cup
    | 80 ml extra-virgin
    olive oil

1 tablespoon brown sugar
    or maple syrup

Fine-grain sea salt

½ teaspoon caraway seeds

1 large clove garlic

1 tablespoon harissa

3 tablespoons freshly
    squeezed lemon juice

A small head of lettuce,
    trimmed

Labneh (see page 321) or
    goat cheese, to serve

Preheat the oven to 350°F | 175°C and adjust the oven rack to the top third of the oven. In a bowl, toss about half the tomatoes gently—but well—with the 2 tablespoons olive oil, the sugar, and a couple of pinches of salt. Arrange them in a single layer, cut side up, on a rimmed baking sheet. Bake, without stirring, until the tomatoes shrink a bit and start to caramelize around the edges, 45 to 60 minutes. Set aside to cool.

In the meantime, toast the caraway seeds in a dry skillet until fragrant. Transfer to a mortar and pestle and crush. Add the garlic clove and a pinch of salt and mash into a paste. Work in the harissa, then the lemon juice, and gradually the remaining ⅓ cup | 80 ml olive oil. When ready to serve, gently toss the roasted and raw tomatoes in a large bowl with about half of the harissa oil and the lettuce. Taste and season with a bit more salt, if needed. Serve topped with a little strained yogurt and the remaining harissa oil on the side.

Quick-Pickled Rose Petals

dried rose petals ✻ white wine vinegar

I tend to keep dried rose petals around and make these now and then for a fragrant addition to couscous or as an accent on fruit salads. The rose-infused vinegar is great as well, and you can do a larger batch for use in shrubs (see page 260). The petals are also a nice punctuation on flatbread slathered with a bit of strained yogurt (see page 321) and green jam (see page 143).

MAKES ¼ CUP | 7 G

¼ cup | 0.25 oz | 7 g
dried rose petals
(see page 312)

¼ cup | 60 ml white wine
vinegar

1 tablespoon plus
1 teaspoon hot water

You can leave the petals whole or chop them a bit. Then combine all of the ingredients in a small bowl. Toss until the petals are saturated and no longer float on top of the liquid. Let sit for at least 30 minutes, but preferably longer—an hour or two yields the best texture. Strain the petals from the vinegar, reserving the vinegar for another use. Serve as a condiment.

Yellow Couscous

saffron * turmeric * golden raisins * almonds

At its finest, couscous should be a tender, fluffy, delicate affair—light grains of rolled wheat steamed and seasoned with whatever you fancy. This version is hand-rubbed with saffron and turmeric, studded with almonds and golden raisins, and feathered with green onions and dill.

(Pictured on the following pages.)

SERVES 4 TO 6

1½ cups | 7.5 oz | 215 g dried couscous

Pinch of saffron (about 20 threads)

½ teaspoon ground turmeric

1 teaspoon fine-grain sea salt

1 tablespoon extra-virgin olive oil, plus more for serving

½ cup | 2 oz | 60 g golden raisins

¾ cup | 4 oz | 115 g coarsely chopped toasted almonds

½ cup | 2 oz | 55 g chopped green onions

¾ cup | 0.75 oz | 20 g stemmed fresh dill

3 oz | 85 g goat cheese, crumbled, or strained yogurt

Place the couscous in a large bowl and rinse in cold water. Strain and rinse a second time. This time allow the couscous to sit, covered with water, for 5 to 10 minutes. Drain, shake off any excess water, and sprinkle the saffron, turmeric, salt, olive oil, and golden raisins across the top of the couscous. Mix the ingredients together with your fingertips, breaking up any lumps along the way. Gently spoon the couscous mixture into a steamer. It is possible to fashion one by using a strainer atop a large pot: the strainer just needs to be fine enough to prevent the couscous from falling through; alternately, you can line the strainer with cheesecloth. Because you want the resulting couscous to be light and fluffy, avoid packing it down in any way.

Fill the bottom third of your pot with water and bring it to a boil over high heat. Once it's boiling, dial the heat back to a simmer, place the couscous-filled steamer on top, cover, and cook for 10 minutes. Uncover and use a fork to fluff—continue to cook, covered, for another 10 minutes, or until the couscous is tender and cooked through. Turn the couscous out onto a platter and fluff again. Sprinkle with the almonds, green onions, and dill, then finish with the goat cheese and a generous drizzle of olive oil.

Roasted Winter Squash

orange * yogurt * cinnamon * ginger

Slathered in warming spices and citrus, this winter squash is roasted to tender, caramelized oblivion. A finishing dollop of tart yogurt and a few cilantro sprigs make it an easy winter warmer. Argan oil can be hard to come by, but its distinctive earthiness is worth seeking out—that said, it's fine to substitute olive oil. There's no need to peel the acorn squash—the skin is beautiful, and when prepared in this fashion, perfectly edible.

SERVES 4 TO 6

1 medium acorn squash

1 teaspoon ground cinnamon

1 teaspoon dried ginger

¾ teaspoon fine-grain sea salt

4 tablespoons | 60 ml argan oil

Zest of ½ orange

Scant ¼ cup | 50 ml freshly squeezed orange juice

½ cup | 120 ml plain yogurt

A handful of cilantro

Preheat the oven to 375°F | 190°C and place the rack in the bottom third.

Cut the squash into eight 1-inch | 2.5cm thick crescent shapes, removing the seeds in the process; place them in a large bowl. In a small bowl, combine the cinnamon, ginger, ½ teaspoon of the salt, 2 tablespoons of the argan oil, the orange zest, and orange juice. Whisk together and then drizzle the mixture across the squash and use your hands to slather and massage it evenly across the wedges. Arrange them in a single layer on a rimmed baking sheet, or in a shallow roasting pan, before placing in the oven.

Bake for 20 minutes or until color starts to develop on the bottoms; flip the squash over and bake for an additional 10 to 20 minutes, until golden and tender throughout. Remove from the oven and allow to cool slightly before arranging on a platter. Stir the remaining ¼ teaspoon of salt into the yogurt and dollop across the wedges, sprinkle with cilantro, and finish by drizzling the remaining 2 tablespoons argan oil across the top.

Prickly Pear Cooler

fresh prickly pear juice ✻ limoncello

*There is a uniqueness to the dusty air of Marrakech. It has
the smell of sweet orange blossoms mingling with the wood
burning in community ovens. In the medina, cedar adds
another note, emanating from shop fixtures and carving
vendors. And all of these are outdone by Yamaha motorbike
exhaust. It's intense, sometimes assaultive, and there are
times when a break is needed and welcome. Regardless of
where you are in the medina, you're not far from a café or
a juice cart. Freshly squeezed orange, lemon, and grapefruit
are most common, but on occasion you'll come across juice of
the prickly pear—you see vendors pushing large carts
of spiked fruits through the souks.*

*The juice of the prickly pear is vibrant and electric pink in
hue. At home, they appear at markets in late summer, often
despined. Once despined, they're easy to peel, and if you chop
the flesh and let it macerate with a touch of brown sugar,
it's easy to press the juice through a strainer. I make this
simple cooler, spiking it with soda water, or something a bit
stronger if the timing is right—limoncello, sambuca,
or vodka are all viable options.*

SERVES 4

6 red prickly pears,
despined

3 teaspoons natural
brown sugar

Ice

Soda water

Vodka, limoncello, or
sambuca (optional)

Peel the prickly pears, roughly chop the flesh, and combine with the sugar in a bowl. Let sit, macerating, for a few
minutes, before smashing with a wooden spoon and pushing the flesh through a strainer. Reserve the juice and discard the solids. Pour 1 to 2 tablespoons of the juice into
4 glasses filled with ice and top each with soda water and
a kiss of vodka, limoncello, or sambuca.

JAPAN

*Tokyo * Kyoto * Koya-san * Naoshima*

IF SAKURA SEASON is the harbinger of spring in Japan, I primarily know the final days of winter. It's the time of year when you might see flurries of snow spiral in tendrils from the heights of a Tokyo skyscraper, while the first precocious camellia blossoms shiver at street level.

Much of my time in Japan is spent walking, sunrise forward, in all but the worst of weather. Substantial scarves, and boots, and hand socks are involved. My first impression of each visit is of the crush of crowds, the rhythmic ebb and flow of people shuttling here and there, up and down—the waves of people moving. Serpentine train tracks and overpasses weave around bouquets of buildings. It's bullet trains, and bejeweled nails, and tiny dogs in vests, and vending machines with choices. Endless choices. And then you settle in and open your eyes to everything that isn't this.

I think of the sound of nightingale floors, and the rhythm of the ginshadan garden sculptures, the intoxicating scent of the season's first white-petaled ume trees, and the flouncy tulle and chiffon skirts on girls in whispery shades of soft pastels. It's the cloudlike tofu, tangles of soba noodles, precision bento boxes, and feather-light tempura that make the lasting impression. The frozen breath of monks chanting in the low light before dawn, and the scent of cedar, and of tatami mats, and of temple incense. It's the welcome bite of sake or sansho pepper, or the Gyokuro green tea warming me from the inside.

My Japanese Pantry

BROWN RICE VINEGAR

DAIKON

GINGER

KINOME

KOMBU

MIRIN

MISO

MITSUBA

MUSHROOMS

NORI

SAKE

SANSHO PEPPER

SHICHIMI TOGARASHI

SHISO

SHOYU

SOBA

SOY MILK

SUDACHI

TOASTED SESAME OIL

TOFU

UMEBOSHI PLUM

WAKAME

WASABI

YUBA

YUZU

Miso Oat Porridge

radish * walnuts * chives

A simple bowl of oats to sit squarely on the savory side of the breakfast spectrum. Well-toasted rolled oats are finished with a bit of miso, then topped with a load of minced chives, walnuts, and baby radishes and a thread of cream. I encourage you to experiment with the miso you use here: it comes in a wonderful spectrum ranging from white to yellow to red to brown. It can be made from rice, barley, buckwheat, soybeans—the list goes on. Just note that some miso is stronger in flavor and saltier than others. You'll want to add miso until the oats are to your liking. The miso acts as the seasoning, so no additional salt is needed.

SERVES 4

1 tablespoon unsalted
 butter

1½ cups | 5 oz | 140 g
 rolled oats

3 cups | 710 ml water

1 to 3 tablespoons miso

Lots of toasted walnuts,
 minced chives, and/or
 shaved radishes,
 for topping

Cream or crème fraîche,
 to finish

Melt the butter in a saucepan over medium heat, stir in the oats, and patiently cook until the oats get well-toasted and fragrant, about 5 minutes. Stir in the water, bring to a simmer, and cook until the water is absorbed, 10 minutes or so. Remove from the heat. Place 1 tablespoon of the miso in a separate bowl and add a few big spoonfuls of the oats. Stir well, then gently but thoroughly fold this miso combination back into the main pot of oats. Taste and adjust with more miso until it is to your liking—if it's properly seasoned with miso, all the flavors will come together.

Serve topped with lots of minced walnuts, chives, and radishes and a good drizzle of cream.

Nori Granola

oats ☀ sesame ☀ cashews ☀ shichimi togarashi

Both sweet and salty, this is an umami-rich homage to the Japanese snack food aisle. Perfect for snacking, it is also a crunchy, satisfying topping for a salad or soup; I even use it to add a top crust to frittatas and omelets on occasion.

Shichimi togarashi is a Japanese spice blend that you can find at some specialty grocers. It typically contains some combination of Sichuan pepper, dried citrus peel, sesame seeds, poppy seeds, hemp seeds, ginger, garlic, shiso, and nori.

MAKES 1 LARGE PAN

¼ cup | 60 ml runny honey

¼ cup | 1.25 oz | 35 g natural cane sugar

2 tablespoons water

3½ cups | 12.5 oz | 350 g rolled oats

½ teaspoon freshly ground black pepper

2 tablespoons whole fennel seeds

¼ cup | 1.5 oz | 40 g sesame seeds

1 tablespoon shichimi togarashi

1½ cups | 6 oz | 170 g coarsely chopped raw cashews

5 (8-inch | 20cm square) sheets of nori, torn and crumbled into irregular 1-inch | 2.5cm pieces

1½ teaspoons fine-grain sea salt

¼ cup | 60 ml extra-virgin olive oil

Preheat the oven to 300°F | 150°C. Line a large, rimmed baking sheet with parchment paper.

In a small saucepan, combine the honey, sugar, and water. Cook over medium-high heat, stirring constantly, until the mixture bubbles at the edges and the sugar has dissolved, about 5 minutes. Remove from the heat and let cool slightly.

In a large bowl, combine the oats, black pepper, fennel seeds, sesame seeds, shichimi togarashi, chopped cashews, and nori. Drizzle with the honey mixture, sprinkle with the salt, and stir thoroughly to coat the oats. Add the olive oil and stir again.

Spread the oat mixture in an even, thin layer on the baking sheet, getting as close as you can to the edges. Toast the granola for 30 to 40 minutes, or until golden brown. After the first 20 minutes, give the granola a gentle stir every 10 minutes or so, paying special attention to the edges, to encourage even browning. Remove from the oven and let cool and crisp up completely before serving. Store in an airtight container for up to 1 week.

Simple Salad

sansho pepper ✳ green onions ✳ shoyu ✳ lemon

*Few take more care when making a simple salad than the
Japanese. Order a green salad in the humblest of cafés and
chances are good you'll be served a vibrant bed of greens
barely tossed with a hint of strong dressing. You get the sense
every leaf was picked through, the best making their way to
your plate. The attention to detail serves to inspire anyone
who makes salads regularly—a reminder that starting with
good greens that are well washed and gently but thoroughly
dried goes a long way in the right direction.*

*As you see here, I don't always bother making a proper
vinaigrette for salads—particularly when I'm using arugula
or other spicy greens like mizuna. Instead, I toss the leaves
with a splash of good olive oil, season well—in this case with
shoyu—and zest with as much lemon peel as I can get away
with. I add shredded green onions and plenty of sansho
pepper. You can use whatever herbs you have on hand,
Japanese or otherwise. I call for shiso, but like it with basil in
the summer (or a combination of both). It's the sort of salad
I tend to enjoy alongside preparations like the Broiled Miso
Tofu (page 175) or the Simmered Winter Squash (page 192)
for a welcome blast of green.*

SERVES 4

4 handfuls | 3 oz | 85 g
arugula or mizuna

A dozen shiso or basil
leaves, thinly slivered

1 tablespoon good olive oil

Scant ½ teaspoon shoyu

Zest of 1 lemon, or more if
you like

⅛ teaspoon sansho pepper

8 green onions, trimmed
and slivered

Just before serving, combine the arugula and shiso in a
bowl. Add the olive oil and give it a good toss, drizzle the
shoyu across the salad, sprinkle over the lemon zest, and
gently toss again. Season with sansho pepper and serve
topped with lots and lots of green onions.

Baby Radishes & Nori Butter

sesame ✳ yuzu ✳ cumin ✳ cayenne

The Japanese pantry puts a range of seaweeds and vegetables to use in all manner of everyday preparations—stock, relishes, wrappers, crackers, snacks, and salads. Fortunately, we also have access to good sea vegetable harvesters along the Northern California coast, and I like to experiment with different ways to put their offerings to use. I've been making this little side dish to serve with Root Donburi (page 196) or Tempeh with Shoyu Butter (page 183). The combination of radishes, butter, and sea salt is classic, but here I pack the butter with crumbled toasted nori, sesame seeds, and spices. The nori butter works beautifully over warm brown rice (see page 309), or tossed with simply blanched or roasted vegetables.

MAKES ½ CUP | 4 OZ | 115 G
BUTTER

12 oz | 340 g baby radishes, washed and trimmed

NORI BUTTER

1 (8-inch | 20cm square) sheet of nori

½ cup | 4 oz | 115 g unsalted butter, at room temperature

¼ teaspoon fine-grain sea salt

¼ teaspoon yuzu or lemon zest

4 teaspoons toasted sesame seeds

¼ teaspoon ground cayenne pepper

½ teaspoon ground toasted cumin

Wash and trim the greens from the radishes, dry well, and arrange on a plate or platter.

To make the compound butter, start by toasting the nori. If you have a gas burner, you can carefully wave it across the flame until it brightens and crisps up. Alternately you can toast it in your oven (at 350°F | 180°C) on a baking sheet, or on a skillet or griddle. Let cool, then crumble and chop into the smallest flecks you can manage. Set aside.

In a bowl, cream the butter using a spoon until light, then add the nori, salt, yuzu, sesame seeds, cayenne, and cumin. Stir until all of the ingredients are evenly distributed. Serve alongside the radishes on a plate or platter.

Broiled Miso Tofu

mitsuba ☀ sansho pepper ☀ sake

One of the things that came as a surprise to me as I began to better understand the Japanese cooking palette was how compelling (and yet unfamiliar) the range of herbs is. Red and green shiso, kinome, and mitsuba, *all unique in their own way, are well worth sourcing (or growing).*

To make a miso glaze for the tofu here, I use mitsuba *as the accent. Referred to as Japanese parsley, and often available in the produce section of Japanese or Asian markets, it has a flavor that is clean and green, with some celery leaf and chervil notes. That said, it can be tough to find outside of a Japanese grocery, and this preparation is also great with basil, cilantro, or chives. I've also used ⅓ cup | 0.5 oz | 15 g of blanched, finely chopped nettles in place of the* mitsuba *leaves, ending up with one of my favorite versions yet.*

SERVES 2 TO 4

12 oz | 340 g extra-firm tofu

1 tablespoon mirin

2 tablespoons sake

¼ cup | 2.5 oz | 70 g sweet white miso

1 egg yolk

A small handful mitsuba leaves or basil or cilantro, plus more for serving

⅛ teaspoon sansho pepper

4 green onions, thinly sliced

Line a baking sheet with parchment paper. Drain any liquid off the tofu and pat completely dry. Slice the block horizontally and then into six equal slabs. Arrange on the baking sheet.

Combine the mirin, sake, miso, and egg yolk in a small saucepan over medium-low heat. Continuously whisking, heat until it thickens to the point that it holds streaks as the whisk runs through—about 160°F | 71°C—thick enough that you can spread it across the tofu and not have it run off. Immediately remove from the heat, transfer to a bowl, and allow the miso mixture to cool a bit. Mince the *mitsuba* extremely finely and stir it in along with the sansho pepper. Taste and adjust to your liking.

Place a rack in the top third of your oven, give each slab of tofu a thick slather of the miso mixture, and place under the broiler until the miso is set and visibly baked. Serve hot or room temp sprinkled with green onions and chopped *mitsuba*.

NOTE: If you make double the miso spread, it's great alongside rice or swirled into an egg scramble. I call for a sweet white miso here, but occasionally add a touch of red or brown miso to add a bit more depth—for example: 3½ tablespoons sweet white miso plus ½ tablespoon red miso.

Turmeric Miso Soup

black pepper ✴ garlic ✴ olive oil

Turmeric is a powerful, health-promoting root used across numerous traditional cultures, and I take notice of how and when it is used in cooking wherever I am. It punctuates different realms of Japanese life, taken by some as a hangover cure and sipped as a tea by others. This is a turmeric-centric take on miso soup and an easy way to incorporate more of it into your day-to-day eating. Depending on what sort of soup you're after, you can prepare this either with or without the hearty chunky vegetables. I often serve it over brown rice or noodles to make a one-bowl meal.

SERVES 4

2 tablespoons extra-virgin olive oil

1 medium fennel bulb, trimmed and chopped

1 large carrot, cut into ½-inch | 1.25cm chunks

1 small yellow onion, quartered

4 cloves garlic, quartered

2 teaspoons freshly ground black pepper

1¼ tablespoons ground turmeric

6 cups | 1.5 L water

3 tablespoons white miso

¾ teaspoon fine-grain sea salt

10 oz | 285 g tofu, cut into small cubes

¼ cup | 0.25 oz | 8 g minced chives

Lemon wedges, to serve

In a saucepan over medium-high heat, combine the olive oil, fennel, carrot, onion, garlic, and black pepper. Stir until coated, then stir in the turmeric, and immediately after, the water. Bring to a boil, then reduce to a gentle simmer for 15 minutes, or until the vegetables are tender. Pour the broth through a fine strainer, then return it to the saucepan over low heat.

At this point, choose whether or not to add the vegetables back to the soup. To make the miso easy to incorporate, stir a splash of the broth into it, then add back to the broth. Since some miso is saltier than others, taste and add salt to your liking. Getting the salt right is important. Stir in the tofu and allow it to heat through. Serve in bowls, topped with minced chives and a generous squeeze of lemon.

Carrot & Sake Salad

sweet lemon dressing * red spring onions

Secluded Koya-san, or Mt. Koya, sits to the south of Nara and is accessed by train followed by a slow scenic climb by cable car through a forest of cedar trees. It is a monastery town— few vehicles and no hotels—and an incredibly special way to explore temple lodging, enjoy shojin-ryori *vegetarian cuisine, and take in the rhythms of monastic life. One of the days we spent exploring the town and temples was numbingly cold, necessitating a retreat into a café along the tiny main street. We had tea and a simple set lunch including one of the more inspiring carrot salads I've had. Bright in color and flavor, with a sweet lemon dressing, this is my approximation of it. Sometimes I grate the carrots as they did; other times I shave slices whisper-thin on a mandoline (as pictured here).*

For cutting the carrots, you can use a food processor with the grating attachment with good results, although hand grating on a box grater gives a nice, defined texture.

SERVES 6

SAKE LEMON DRESSING

1 tablespoon sake

1½ tablespoons natural brown sugar

⅓ cup | 80 ml freshly squeezed lemon juice

Scant ½ teaspoon fine-grain salt

2 tablespoons sunflower, sesame, or olive oil

---

2 cups | 9 oz | 255 g seeds or nuts, such as sunflower seeds, pepitas, or pine nuts

2 teaspoons sunflower or extra-virgin olive oil

⅛ teaspoon fine-grain salt

1 pound / 455 g carrots, grated or very thinly shaved

½ small cucumber, halved, seeded, smashed a bit, then chopped

8 small red spring onions or green onions, thinly sliced

Lemon zest

Preheat the oven to 350°F | 175°C.

While the oven is heating, make the sake lemon dressing. Whisk together the sake, brown sugar, lemon juice,

and salt, then whisk in the oil. Taste and adjust if needed. It should be sweet with a lemony bite. Set aside until ready to serve.

Toss the seeds with the oil and salt and arrange in a single layer on a baking sheet. Bake for about 10 minutes, turning a couple of times along the way to get even browning. If you're using pine nuts, keep an extra close eye on them. Set aside to cool.

Just before serving, place the carrots in a serving bowl with the cucumber and most of the onions and seeds. Pour two-thirds of the dressing over the carrots and toss well. Taste, decide if you'd like more dressing, and if you would, add some and toss again. Serve topped with the remaining seeds and onions and some lemon zest.

Variations: On occasion I do a toasted sesame version of this salad, swapping in toasted sesame oil in place of 1 tablespoon of the olive/sunflower oil in the dressing.

Also, feel free to play around with different carrot varietals. Here I use heirloom rainbow carrots, but go with what you like or have on hand.

Tempeh with Shoyu Butter

shoyu * green onion * sesame seeds

While many people hit up ramen shops, sushi counters, and yakitori spots while in Japan, I find myself seeking out macrobiotic-leaning cafés, soba specialists, and shojin-ryori *practitioners. I didn't really appreciate how good tempeh could be until I tasted it, on one of my first days in Japan, at one of the unassuming cafés in the heart of Tokyo. Simply adorned, the tempeh was light and nutty and didn't need much accompaniment.*

To get away with a simply prepared tempeh dish takes some consideration—buy good organic tempeh with nice visual appeal and go from there. For this version, a quick steam really opens the tempeh up, and you don't need much beyond that: a simple soy butter and a fresh vegetable—whatever is in season, really. I use cabbage here, but have done versions with broccolini and kale.

SERVES 2

8 oz | 225 g tempeh

3 tablespoons unsalted butter

2 tablespoons shoyu

Scant 1 tablespoon brown sugar

1 tablespoon water

1 small napa cabbage (10 oz | 285 g), cored and sliced into ¼-inch | 6mm ribbons

5 green onions, thinly sliced

1 tablespoon toasted sesame seeds

Slice the tempeh into 12 thin triangles and steam it, covered, over simmering water, for 10 minutes.

Once the tempeh is steamed, combine the butter, shoyu, sugar, and water in a large skillet over medium-high heat. When hot, stir in the cabbage, toss well, and sauté for about 40 seconds, just long enough for the cabbage to start to collapse. Add the tempeh and toss gently until coated, another 30 seconds or so; remove from the heat. Immediately transfer to a serving platter or bowl, sprinkle with green onions and sesame seeds, toss once or twice, and enjoy.

Plum Wine Sparkler

prosecco ∗ plum wine

Originally taken as a medicinal drink, the Japanese plum wines (umeshu) *I've tasted tend to be sweet and aromatic, with a hint of salty sourness. It's made from steeping ume fruit while still green in alcohol and sugar, and while many enjoy it on the rocks or straight, I tend to like it as an accent in drinks. For example, this quick, effervescent sparkler goes down easy. It's a touch offbeat, and it introduces an unfamiliar flavor that is hard to put a finger on, in a good way.*

You can find Japanese plum wine next to the sake in many stores with a decent Japanese selection. For a lower alcohol version, mix the plum wine with tonic or sparkling water in place of the prosecco.

MAKES 1 SERVING

1 tablespoon plum wine   ⅓ cup | 80 ml prosecco

Be sure both wines are well chilled before serving. Add the plum wine to whatever glass you like to drink sparkling wine from, and top with the prosecco. Make to order, and enjoy immediately.

Sake-Glazed Mushrooms

sun-dried tomatoes * herbs

I love to use nameko mushrooms here, but regular brown mushrooms work wonderfully as well. Look for sun-dried tomatoes that are plump and pliable—either dry (sold in a bag) or packed in oil. If you can find only sun-dried tomatoes packed in herb oil, it's not a problem; simply give them a quick rinse, pat dry, and proceed with chopping. Also, if you want to make more mushrooms than this recipe yields, make two separate batches to avoid crowding the pan.

SERVES 2 TO 4

8 oz | 225 g mushrooms

2 tablespoons unsalted butter

Fine-grain sea salt

¼ cup | 60 ml sake

1½ tablespoons chopped sun-dried tomato

10 shiso or basil leaves, shredded

Prep the mushrooms by brushing them with a damp cloth or paper towel if they need a bit of cleaning. Cut the mushrooms and stems into bite-size (1-inch | 2.5cm) pieces.

Melt the butter in a large skillet over high heat. When the butter has melted, add the mushrooms with a couple of pinches of salt. Toss the mushrooms to coat with the butter and salt, make sure they're in a single layer, and leave them alone for a minute or so. The mushrooms should release some of their liquid and start to brown. Shake the pan and toss the mushrooms with a metal spatula, then leave alone again until you get more browning. The mushrooms should be close to finished now. Dial back the heat, wait about 10 seconds for the pan to cool a bit, then carefully add the sake and most of the sun-dried tomatoes. Cook until the sake is absorbed, another 20 seconds or so, remove from the heat, and stir in most of the shiso. Serve topped with the remaining tomatoes and shiso.

Watermelon Radish Soup

nettles * fresh ginger juice * silken tofu

This soup is all about the broth. And if you hit the mark, it should make you glow from the inside. I encountered numerous versions of strong, savory ginger broth while in Japan and have come to think of them as small bowls of invigoration—staving off cold weather and ill health in general. Watermelon radish bestows a lovely rosy color to the broth and is worth seeking out. Use tongs, dish towels, or gloves when handling the raw nettles, as they sting until well cooked.

SERVES 4

1 pound | 455 g silken tofu

6 cups | 1.5 L water

2 cups | 8 oz | 225 g watermelon radish, peeled and cut into ¼-inch | 6mm dice, plus more, thinly sliced, to serve

5 large kale leaves (or equivalent quantity of nettles), stemmed and finely chopped

3½ tablespoons fresh ginger juice (page 316)

1½ teaspoons fine-grain sea salt

6 green onions, thinly sliced

Black sesame seeds, to serve

Fashion a double boiler using a stainless steel bowl placed over a smaller saucepan of simmering water. Gently place the tofu in the stainless steel bowl, cover, and heat through while you're working through the rest of the recipe. You want the tofu to be warm when it is combined with the hot broth later on in the process.

In a saucepan over medium-high heat, bring the water to a simmer. Add the watermelon radish and cook until tender, 7 to 10 minutes. Stir in the kale, ginger juice, and salt and continue to simmer for a couple of minutes more.

To serve, spoon a bit of warm silken tofu into each bowl. Ladle in the hot broth and radishes and garnish with green onions, slices of watermelon radish, and a sprinkling of black sesame seeds.

Variation: For a more substantial meal, serve over brown rice or soba noodles.

Brussels Sprouts

Japanese mustard ✳ walnuts ✳ yuzu

Karashi, *or Japanese mustard, is hot and direct. It comes in a few different forms—tube or powder—and it's great with brussels sprouts. If Japanese mustard is hard to come by, any spicy yellow mustard will get you in the neighborhood. I make these and either serve them on their own, or pile them atop soba noodles or brown rice. Adding tofu or shredded tempeh to the skillet makes a simple one-pan meal of them, and a thread of spicy, cold-pressed mustard seed oil drizzled prior to serving is great if you happen to have some on hand. When shopping for brussels sprouts, seek out the small, tight ones.*

You can make the dressing ahead of time, keeping it on hand for a few days, and it can be doubled or tripled.

SERVES 4

12 oz | 340 g brussels sprouts

½ tablespoon sesame oil

Fine-grain sea salt

⅓ cup | 1.25 oz | 35 g walnuts, toasted

SPICY MUSTARD DRESSING

2 tablespoons sesame oil

1 tablespoon sake

1 tablespoon freshly squeezed yuzu or lemon juice

½ teaspoon shoyu

½ to 1 teaspoon karashi (Japanese mustard)

Scant teaspoon of runny honey (optional)

Wash the brussels sprouts. Trim the stem ends and remove any raggy outer leaves. Cut in quarters or halves from stem to top and toss in a bowl with the sesame oil. Set aside.

To make the dressing, whisk together the sesame oil, sake, yuzu juice, shoyu, and ½ teaspoon of mustard. If you like more spiciness, add mustard a bit at a time to taste. If you need a bit of sweetness to balance things out, work in a small amount of honey. Set aside.

To cook the sprouts, place your largest skillet over medium heat. Don't overheat the skillet, or the outsides of the sprouts will cook too quickly. Place the sprouts in the pan, sprinkle with a couple of pinches of salt, cover, and cook for roughly 3 minutes; the sprouts should show only a hint of browning. Cut into a sprout to gauge whether they're tender. If not, cover and cook for a few more minutes. Once they are just tender, uncover, turn up the heat, and cook until the flat sides of the sprouts are deep brown and caramelized. Toss them to get some browning on the rounded side. Transfer to a serving bowl and toss with about half of the dressing. Taste and add more dressing if you like.

Serve topped with the walnuts.

Simmered Winter Squash

lemon ✳ garlic chives ✳ shoyu

I make this constantly when winter squash floods the markets. Simmered squash (kabocha no nimono) is a much-loved side dish in many Japanese homes. It's simple and satisfying, and best of all, there's no need to peel the squash. In fact, that would be exactly what you don't want to do. The skin lends just the right amount of structure, as well as lovely contrasting color and texture. Departing from traditional versions, I added some white beans I had on hand to the pot one night, and that version stuck.

Kabocha squash is pictured here, but I have equal fondness for red kuri and delicata squashes. You can leave the peels on all of these.

SERVES 4

2 pounds | 900 g winter squash

2 cups | 480 ml water, dashi, or lightly salted broth

2 tablespoons muscovado or brown sugar

2 tablespoons mirin

2 tablespoons shoyu, plus more for serving

1½ cups | 10.5 oz | 300 g large white beans, cooked (optional)

2 tablespoons extra-virgin olive oil

Zest of 1 lemon

½ cup | 0.75 oz | 20 g chopped nira (garlic chives), green onions, or chives

Sea salt, for serving (optional)

Wash the squash well and cut, seed, and slice it into 1½-inch | 4cm chunks of equal thickness. Combine the water, sugar, mirin, and shoyu in a saucepan. Stir to combine, taste, and tweak (with more shoyu, for example) until it tastes nice. Add the squash and jiggle the pan a bit to level everything out. Bring the mixture to a boil, then simmer over low heat for about 15 minutes, or until the squash is tender throughout and the skin is cooked through. Stir in the beans and let them heat through.

To serve, use a slotted spoon to transfer the squash to a shallow bowl or platter. Drizzle with a bit of shoyu and the olive oil and sprinkle with zest and garlic chives. Depending on the sweetness of the squash, you'll want to salt accordingly—either with more shoyu or with sea salt.

Variation: When nettles are available, I stir in ⅔ cup | 1 oz | 30 g of chopped, blanched nettles along with the beans.

Soy Milk Dressing

thick soy milk * olive oil * garlic

Light yet creamy, this is a simple, all-purpose dressing to use on everything from steamed vegetables to grain salads. This is the base recipe, but it welcomes variations—lots of chopped, fresh herbs, spices, or crumbled toasted seaweed. The key here is tracking down good, thick, real, pure soy milk. Soy milk made from organic soy beans and water—minus the sweeteners, stabilizers, and flavorings you often see on soy milk cartons.

MAKES 1 CUP

1 medium clove garlic

1 teaspoon fine-grain sea salt

¾ cup | 180 ml thick soy milk

2½ tablespoons brown rice vinegar

¼ cup | 60 ml extra-virgin olive oil

Mingle the garlic and salt on a cutting board and mash into a paste using the flat side of your knife, then chop. Place in a bowl or jar, then add the soy milk and vinegar. Combine with a whisk and let sit for 5 minutes or so. Gradually whisk in the olive oil. Taste and adjust with more salt, vinegar, or soy milk. Use immediately or refrigerate for up to 2 days.

Shiso Gin & Tonic

lime ✳ lemon ✳ tonic

I think of shiso as a summer herb, though the green varietal tends to be available in Asian markets year-round. An easy-to-grow, aromatic member of the mint family, it can be used in many of the ways you might use mint or basil in other culinary preparations—shredded over noodles or rice, pounded into a sauce or paste, or, as here, infused into a drink. It works beautifully alongside gin's botanical notes, and I like to use it in this simple twist on a classic gin and tonic. You can use any leftover syrup in lemonade or limeade, tossed with fruit, or drizzled over yogurt. I opt for the flavor (and color) neutrality of cane sugar here, but if you're looking to avoid sugar, you can replace it with honey in the shiso simple syrup.

MAKES ABOUT 1 CUP | 240 ML SYRUP

SHISO SIMPLE SYRUP

20 shiso leaves, torn

1 cup | 240 ml water

⅓ cup | 2.5 oz | 70 g natural cane sugar

Zest of 1 lemon

Zest of 1 lime

Gin

Ice cubes

Tonic water

To make the shiso simple syrup, in a saucepan over gentle heat, slowly bring the shiso, water, sugar, and lemon and lime zest barely to a simmer, stirring until the sugar is dissolved. Try to avoid boiling—you want to infuse the syrup, not overcook the shiso. Remove from the heat and let the shiso steep at room temperature, covered, for 20 to 30 minutes. Transfer to an airtight glass jar and chill until cold. If you're pressed for time, place the jar in the freezer until chilled but not frozen. Strain the syrup through a sieve into a bowl, pressing then discarding the solids. The syrup will keep, refrigerated, for 4 to 5 days.

To make each drink, combine ¼ cup | 2 oz | 60 ml of gin and 2 teaspoons of shiso syrup in each glass (I use little Picardie glasses here). Stir to combine, fill each glass two-thirds full with ice, and top off with ¼ cup | 2 oz | 60 ml of tonic water. Stir again and taste, and add a bit more tonic water if you like.

NOTE: If you can get your hands on red shiso, it makes a stunner of a variation here. Follow the same instructions, but give the red shiso simple syrup a good squeeze of lime juice after straining to really boost the ruby color.

Root Donburi

sesame * pickled cucumber * sweet potato *
rice * carrots

Donburi is a Japanese rice bowl preparation. Think of it as a generous bowl of (brown) rice topped with neighborhoods of ingredients arranged on top. The nature of a preparation like this is heavy on the components, but you can always make extra to have available throughout the rest of your week. The carrots are great tossed with tofu, and the umeboshi cucumbers are a nice sandwich or spring roll addition. Be sure to use a box cutter to grate the carrots, rather than a Microplane grater, which will shred them too fine.

To toast the nori, gently wave it over a gas burner until it crinkles and shifts color a bit, or toast it in an oven.

SERVES 4

2 tablespoons brown rice vinegar

1 tablespoon honey

1 tablespoon plus ½ teaspoon shoyu

2½ cups | 15 oz | 425 g cooked brown rice (see page 309), warm

2 tablespoons toasted sesame seeds

2 medium carrots, grated

2 tablespoons sunflower or sesame oil

1 medium cucumber, seeded and thinly sliced

1 tablespoon umeboshi plum paste

2 medium sweet potatoes, peeled and cut into ¼-inch | 6mm cubes

8 oz | 225 g extra-firm tofu, drained, cut into ¼-inch | 6mm cubes

2 sheets toasted nori, crumbled

1 cup | 4 oz | 115 g green onions, thinly sliced

In a small bowl, stir together the vinegar, honey, and shoyu. Pour half of this mixture over the rice while it's still warm; mix well, cover, and set aside.

In a small bowl, combine the sesame seeds, carrots, 1 tablespoon of the oil, and the remaining ½ teaspoon shoyu. Stir to combine and set aside. In another small bowl, combine the cucumber with the umeboshi paste and massage with your hands to combine.

In a large skillet over medium-high heat, combine the remaining 1 tablespoon oil with the sweet potatoes. Toss to coat, cover, and sauté for a few minutes, stirring regularly, until the potatoes are golden and tender throughout. Push the potatoes to the side and add the tofu to the pan. Cook until the tofu takes on a bit of color and is heated through, about 7 minutes. Remove from the heat.

To serve, add a generous portion of rice to each bowl. Arrange neighborhoods of carrots, cucumber, and sweet potato tofu over the rice. Top each bowl with crumbled nori and green onions. Serve with the remaining sauce, allowing each person to season to their liking.

ITALY

Rome ✶ Naples ✶ Palermo ✶ Ischia ✶ Bisceglie ✶ Umbria

AEROPORTO INTERNAZIONALE LEONARDO DA VINCI DI FIUMICINO was my first European passport stamp. I was twenty-four, had perhaps $400 in the bank, and was about to fall hard for Italy. It wasn't just the buildings and architecture, or the famous sights; it was more than that—it was the *ti amo* graffiti and the lyric Italian voices spilling from open windows, the familiar mingling of young and old, and the buildings that were able to take my imagination backward, seemingly forever. It was mirrored aviator glasses, massive porcini mushrooms, piazzas both tiny and expansive, theatrical fountains, church bells at dawn, and the endless marble pockmarked by thousands of years of weather, war, and passersby.

Over the years my preoccupation with Italy has happily robbed me of visits to a host of other cities and countries. I return regularly, often forgoing other perfectly enticing destinations. I've driven from Lazio through Umbria, east to the coast and then south through Le Marche. I've watched the fishermen slowly make their way toward shore at dawn on the Puglian coast and tasted the wild-picked greens of the region. I've soaked in the mineral-rich springs of Ischia and rested my head in an old, tarnished hotel in Naples with a view of the sea, placid and blue, punctuated with cottonball clouds. There were late night strolls through the shadowed streets of Palermo, and sun-soaked bike rides on the deserted island roads of Favignana.

Morning is my favorite time of day there. Crisscrossing towns and cities on foot just after daybreak is one of the things I never tire of. It's quiet, and if you catch it right, you witness the entire city waking up. The smell of the bakeries working full-tilt seeps into the air, though their metal doors are still locked up tight. In Rome, you can weave your way through warrens of narrow cobblestone streets from one neighborhood to the next. Or let your stride stretch along the sidewalks above the Tiber. You can sit at the foot of the Pantheon with no one else around save the pigeons. And, in summer, a morning start saves you from the hot air rising in ripples off the scorched concrete and cobblestone.

My last visit spanned nearly a month, and I never ventured from Rome proper. People-watching easily becomes a preoccupation, and I'd sit for long stretches near husky-voiced *nonnas* at lunch, while they ate, smoked, and laughed in the shade, late into the afternoon.

My Italian Pantry

AMARO

ARUGULA

BALSAMIC VINEGAR

BASIL

BEANS

BERRIES

BURRATA

CAPERS

CITRUS

DRIED FRUIT

EGG PASTA

ESPRESSO

FARRO

FENNEL

GARLIC

HAZELNUTS

HONEY

KALE

LENTILS

MARJORAM

MASCARPONE

MOZZARELLA

OLIVE OIL

OLIVES

PARMIGIANO-REGGIANO

PARSLEY

PEARLED BARLEY

PECORINO

PINE NUTS

PORCINI

PROSECCO

RADICCHIO

RICOTTA

ROMANESCO

ROSEMARY

SAGE

TARRAGON

TOMATOES

VERMOUTH

WINE VINEGARS

Farro Salad

green olives ✳ walnuts ✳ green onions ✳
golden raisins

The farro salad you most often encounter in Italy goes something like this—farro, tomatoes, herbs, cheese, olive oil, and perhaps a splash of vinegar. This is my attempt to take things in a different direction.

Chopped green olives, chives, toasted walnuts, and honey combine with a few other ingredients into a quirky yet delicious preparation that leaves a huge impression. Massive Sicilian Castelvetrano olives are my choice here, but any great-tasting green olives will do—Cerignola, Lucques, or Sevillano—preferably from an olive bar, not a can. If you prepare the olive mixture the day or two ahead of time, it is even better, but bring it to room temperature before serving.

SERVES 6

1¼ cups | 8 oz | 225 g whole or semipearled farro

3 cups | 710 ml water

Fine-grain sea salt

1 pound | 455 g green olives, rinsed then pitted

4 to 6 tablespoons | 60 to 90 ml extra-virgin olive oil

1 cup | 3 oz | 90 g chopped toasted walnut halves

4 to 6 green onions, trimmed and chopped

1 bunch chives, minced

Scant ½ teaspoon crushed red pepper flakes

1 tablespoon honey

2 tablespoons freshly squeezed lemon juice

⅓ cup | 2.5 oz | 70 g golden raisins, chopped

Shaved pecorino cheese, to serve

Combine the farro, water, and ½ teaspoon of salt in a saucepan over medium-high heat. Cover and bring to a boil, then lower the heat to take from a boil to a simmer, and simmer gently for about 15 minutes if semipearled, longer if whole. Cook until tender, but not so long that the grains become mushy. Drain off any extra water and set aside.

Coarsely chop the olives and place them in a bowl along with the olive oil, walnuts, green onions, chives, red pepper flakes, honey, lemon juice, raisins, and ½ teaspoon of salt. Stir well and set aside (or refrigerate) until ready to serve the salad.

The olive mixture is best at room temperature, so if you've refrigerated it, set it out for 30 minutes before doing the final toss. Combine the farro and olive mixture in a bowl and mix to combine well. Taste and add more salt or lemon juice if needed. Serve topped with thin strips of shaved pecorino.

Ricotta Crespelle

milk * eggs * sea salt

Buying fresh ricotta nearly every day in Rome is part of my routine there. It doesn't get any better than ricotta di pecora (made with sheep's milk), plain, with a dusting of salt, spread on something crunchy. That said, these are a standout as well— a version of ricotta crepes, or crespelle. Don't feel compelled to limit them to breakfast.

If you can't find whole wheat pastry flour, make them with all-purpose flour to keep things light. Serve with a side of crisp, just-blanched vegetables or with a dollop of something creamy. Leftover batter cooks up great the day after.

MAKES 4 TO 6 CRESPELLE

1 cup | 8.5 oz | 240 g whole milk ricotta

1 cup plus 2 tablespoons | 270 ml milk

3 large eggs, separated, room temperature

1 cup | 4 oz | 115 g whole wheat pastry flour

1 teaspoon non-aluminum baking powder

Scant ½ teaspoon fine-grain sea salt

Butter, for the pan

In a large bowl, mix the ricotta, milk, and egg yolks until smooth. Sift the flour, baking powder, and salt into another bowl. Add the flour mixture to the ricotta and stir until just barely combined; it's fine if the batter is still a bit floury. Mix the egg whites into the batter with a spatula with as few strokes as possible.

Heat a griddle or pan over medium-low heat, melt a bit of butter in it, then spoon ¼ cup of batter into the pan and tilt the pan, or use the back of a ladle, to guide the batter around the pan. You want to cook it slowly, until the crespelle is deeply golden on one side and the batter is set on top. Fold in half and transfer to a plate to serve immediately. Alternately, you can cook both sides. Repeat until you've worked through all the batter. Sometimes I get two pans going at once.

NOTE: For fluffy ricotta pancakes, whip the egg whites to stiff peaks before folding into the batter.

Radicchio Salad

coriander * pecorino * walnuts * dried figs

Bold color and a back note of bitterness make radicchio a celebratory way to break out of the green salad rut. Here I like to offset the chicory-arugula bite with a bit of sweetness from slivers of dried fig and a touch of cream.

SERVES 4 TO 6

Juice of 1 lemon

Fine-grain sea salt

1 teaspoon honey or sugar

½ teaspoon finely crushed whole coriander seed

⅓ cup | 80 ml extra-virgin olive oil

1 teaspoon heavy cream (optional)

4.5 oz | 125 g arugula, shredded

1 medium head radicchio (about 10 oz | 285 g), cored, and shredded into ¼-inch | 6mm ribbons

1½ cups | 4.5 oz | 125 g walnut halves, toasted and cooled

3 oz | 85 g pecorino cheese

3.5 oz | 100 g dried figs, stemmed, then sliced

Start by combining the lemon juice, ¼ teaspoon of salt, the honey, and coriander in a bowl. Stir to combine. Gradually whisk in the olive oil, followed by the heavy cream. Taste and adjust with more salt, lemon juice, or sugar if needed. Set aside.

Just before serving, combine the arugula, radicchio, and walnuts in a large bowl. Toss with two-thirds of the dressing until well coated. Add most of the pecorino cheese and dried figs and more dressing if needed and gently toss again. Finish with the remaining pecorino and the dried figs.

Grilled Porcini

sage * parsley * olive oil

Make this with market porcini when in Italy, and something less spendy when at home. King trumpets or slabs of portobello are both good alternatives. And when you are herb rich but mushroom poor, the salsa verde is a nice addition to just about any egg preparation, or fold it into potato salad or toss it with anything from asparagus to broccoli to cauliflower. It's also great served over a big family-style platter of mashed potatoes during the holiday season.

SERVES 4

SALSA VERDE

2 small shallots, minced

2 tablespoons white wine vinegar, or to cover

5 tablespoons | 75 ml extra-virgin olive oil, plus more for brushing mushrooms

½ cup | 0.75 oz | 20 g fresh sage leaves (about 1 bunch)

¼ cup | 0.25 oz | 8 g finely chopped parsley leaves

Fine-grain sea salt

---

12 oz | 340 g fresh porcini mushrooms

Extra-virgin olive oil, for brushing

To make the salsa verde, place the shallots in a small bowl, cover with the vinegar, and set aside. Heat 2 tablespoons of the olive oil in a small saucepan over medium heat and fry the sage in 3 or 4 batches—make sure they aren't at all wet when they hit the oil. You'll want to fry the leaves until they shrivel a bit, 15 seconds or so. Place them on a clean dish towel to drain, cool, and crisp up. Once cool, chop the sage leaves and place them, along with the parsley, in a small bowl. Just before serving, drain the vinegar from the shallots and add them to the herb mixture along with the remaining 3 tablespoons of olive oil. Season with a couple pinches of salt, to taste.

Clean the mushrooms if needed with a damp cloth and slice into ½-inch | 1.2cm thick slabs. Brush with a bit of olive oil, place on a medium-hot grill, and cook until golden—3 minutes or so on each side. Alternatively, you can cook these on a rimmed baking sheet under a broiler, flipping once in the process, until deeply browned.

Serve immediately drizzled with the salsa verde.

Fiasco-Style Fagioli

cannellini beans * sage * garlic * red pepper flakes

While struggling with the language, I still manage to accumulate a sizable stack of magazines when in Italy. I love the photos, and the recipes are usually simple enough to decipher. A version of the much loved, Tuscan bean recipe— fagioli al fiasco—was featured in one glossy, and I've been making this version of it ever since. Here's how it works. Traditionally, beans were baked overnight in a Chianti bottle placed near the dying embers of that night's fire. While not exactly authentic, I do a riff on this using my oven and an enamel-lined casserole (or ovenproof pot). It's incredibly simple, yet the beans bake beautifully—luxe, tender, creamy. The fragrant broth is freckled with olive oil and develops a remarkable amount of flavor. These beans are special.

I call for cannellini beans here but regularly do versions with either dried cranberry or cassoulet beans. You can serve the beans on their own, use them to top bruschetta, or ladle over stuffed pasta. The recipe here is a bit more brothy than is typical, but it allows me to make leftovers into an amazing stew—add a bit more water and some cooked farro or rice, then season and top with some grated cheese.

SERVES 6 TO 8

1 pound | 455 g dried cannellini beans, soaked overnight

6 cups | 1.5 L water

½ cup | 120 ml olive oil

5 medium cloves garlic, smashed

7 medium sage leaves

½ teaspoon red pepper flakes

Scant 1 teaspoon fine-grain sea salt

Preheat oven to 225°F | 110°C, with a rack in the bottom. Drain and rinse the beans and place them in a large ovenproof casserole or pot. Add the water, olive oil, garlic, sage, and red pepper flakes and bring to a simmer on the stove top. Remove from the heat, cover, leaving a tiny crack, then transfer to the oven.

Bake for 2 hours, or until the beans are plump and tender. Along the way you want the beans to gently bubble and simmer. Check on them after a few minutes, and if you need to, adjust your oven up to 250°F | 120°C. Stir in the salt after 90 minutes and finish baking. Serve hot or at room temperature.

Fennel Frond Orzo

capers ✳ fennel fronds ✳ almonds ✳ black olives

The key here is pasta shape. Seek out dried pasta, the smaller the better. My favorite is orzo, either whole wheat or a blend of whole wheat and white all-purpose. Fregola, the toasted Sardinian pasta, works nicely as well—all the little dressing bits cling to its raggy surface. In either case, you want a generous ratio of sauce to pasta. The olive mixture can be made in advance and will keep refrigerated, the flavor improving day over day, for a few days covered with a layer of olive oil. Also, while the fennel frond and olive paste is great over pasta, it also makes a sophisticated addition to blanched asparagus or corn just off the grill; or work it into egg salad in place of mayo.

SERVES 4 TO 6

8 oz | 225 g whole wheat orzo

1 thick slice of country bread, crust removed

2 tablespoons white wine vinegar

1 medium clove garlic

½ teaspoon fine-grain sea salt

1 teaspoon whole coriander seeds, toasted

3 tablespoons capers, rinsed

½ cup | 2 oz | 55 g almonds

⅓ cup | 0.25 oz | 8 g chopped garlic chives or green onions

½ cup | 0.75 oz | 20 g finely chopped fennel fronds

10 pitted black olives

⅓ cup | 80 ml olive oil

1 small head radicchio, cored and shredded

Bring a large pot of water to a boil, salt the water generously, and cook the orzo per the package instructions.

In the meantime, make the sauce. Place the bread in a shallow bowl, sprinkle the vinegar on it, and set aside. Pound the garlic with the salt in a mortar along with the coriander seeds until it becomes a paste. In a pinch, you can use the flat side of a knife here, but you'll have to grind the coriander seeds ahead of time. One after another, work in the capers, almonds, garlic chives, fennel fronds, and olives. Pound until the mixture has a chunky texture. Work the bread into the mixture, and then the olive oil, little by little, until the sauce comes together. Taste for vinegar and salt, adding a hint of each if needed. Toss with the orzo and radicchio before turning out into a bowl or serving platter.

Brown Butter Tortelli

balsamic vinegar * lemon zest * spicy greens

This recipe is all about getting your hands on good, freshly made, stuffed pasta. I use a dozen big, chubby, fresh tortelli here, but you can certainly use ravioli—which tends to be much easier to come by, particularly if you're not in Italy, where pasta shops pepper the neighborhoods. Part of their charm is offering the choice of a beautiful range of shapes and fillings that often change throughout the week. The browned butter balsamic sauce here goes nicely with ricotta-stuffed pasta, though in the colder months, substituting pasta filled with winter squash or pumpkin is a swap I encourage. This recipe serves two, but you can easily double or triple it to feed more.

SERVES 2

1 dozen large, fresh tortelli

¼ cup | 2 oz | 60 g unsalted butter

1 tablespoon aged balsamic vinegar

Fine-grain sea salt

Grated zest of 1 lemon

2 or 3 big handfuls of torn arugula or other bitter/spicy greens

Plenty of grated fresh pecorino or Parmesan cheese

Bring a large pot of well-salted water to a boil. Cook the tortelli per the package instructions, or until the pasta floats. Then drain, reserving a small cup of the pasta water.

In the meantime, place the butter in a skillet or saucepan over medium heat. Cook until the butter has browned and is very fragrant and nutty smelling. Remove from the heat and let it cool off for a minute or so. Whisk in the vinegar, a couple of pinches of salt, and most of the lemon zest.

Add the cooked pasta to the pan and toss gently. Add a tiny, tiny splash of the reserved pasta water and toss again. Add the arugula, then turn out immediately into individual bowls or onto a serving platter, and top with a bit of cheese and the remaining lemon zest.

Eggs in Purgatory—Two Ways

cauliflower * tomatoes * marjoram

There are two seasons of eggs in purgatory, or uova al Purgatorio. I do one version in winter with canned crushed tomatoes. The summer version (see Variation) is a beauty featuring chopped yellow tomatoes and toasted almonds. Both are rustic, satisfying one-pan meals appropriate for any time of day and always a favorite family-style preparation. You can substitute other vegetables—romanesco, broccoli, potatoes, and so on —just be sure they're cooked through before adding them to the skillet. It's also okay if florets break free from the cauliflower slabs—just toss them in the flour and go. That said, the more flat surface area you have, the more delicious browning you'll get. For both versions, you will need a large, wide skillet—10 inches | 25 cm at least.

SERVES 2 TO 4

10 oz | 285 g cauliflower florets, (about 1 medium head), cut into ½-inch | 1.2cm slabs

½ cup | 2 oz | 60 g all-purpose or whole wheat pastry flour

¼ cup | 60 ml extra-virgin olive oil

Fine-grain sea salt

¼ teaspoon red pepper flakes

1 (14-oz | 400g) can crushed tomatoes

3 or 4 eggs

20 fresh marjoram leaves

Boil the cauliflower in a pot of salted water for about a minute, until just barely tender. Drain, shake off any extra water, and toss in a large, shallow bowl with the flour. Tap off any extra flour and arrange the slices on a plate until ready to use.

Heat the olive oil in a large skillet over medium-high heat. Arrange the cauliflower in a single layer and cook until deeply golden, 4 to 5 minutes, flipping once to get color on both sides. Stir ¼ teaspoon of salt and the red pepper into the tomatoes before adding to the pan. Give the pan a good shake to distribute the sauce evenly and get it into the pockets. Bring to a simmer, then use a spoon to make little pockets for the eggs near the outer edges of the skillet. Gently break the eggs into the pockets, cover, and cook until the eggs are set—5 minutes or so. Serve in the skillet, sprinkled with the marjoram.

Variation: For the summer version, use 1 pound | 455 g ripe yellow tomatoes instead of the canned tomatoes: chop them into very small pieces, retaining all of the juices. Stir in the salt and red pepper flakes. When you add the tomatoes to the pan, sprinkle the zest of 1 small lemon over top of the tomatoes. Substitute other fresh herbs and herb flowers for all or part of the marjoram, if you like, then finish by sprinkling a small handful of toasted almond slices over the top of the dish.

Vermouth & Seltzer

Italian vermouth ∗ seltzer water ∗ citrus

*When I've had enough chilled Lillet and rosé for the summer,
I switch to this: an Americano minus the Campari. It's
an easy drinking, low-alcohol shim, and just the thing if
you're after a moderate lunchtime cocktail. The version I
saw printed in a vermouth advertisement in a 1940s issue of
Life magazine holds up as simple and unfussed—straight
vermouth, two ice cubes, a thin slice of orange, and
a twist of lemon peel.*

*Your choice of glass is key. Opt for something not too tall,
not too short, not too wide, and certainly not overly fancy. Go
for a dry, white Italian vermouth. You'll have many options
in Italy, less elsewhere; part of the fun is experimenting with
lesser-known vermouths. More broadly distributed, extra dry
Cinzano seems to be the most readily available stateside, and
Boissiere, with its floral notes, is worth seeking out as well. I
like a ratio of four parts vermouth to one part seltzer water.
In a small glass it shapes up like this.*

SERVES 1

Ice cubes

¼ cup dry, white vermouth

1 tablespoon seltzer water

Thin slice of orange,
to garnish

Place 3 or 4 ice cubes in a small glass. Add the vermouth,
top with the seltzer water, and stir. Garnish with the
orange slice.

Biscottini

cornmeal * fennel seeds * rosemary *
lemon zest * limoncello

*Baby biscotti flecked
with rosemary, lemon
zest, and fennel seeds—
you'll be hard-pressed to
find a more fragrant cookie.
And, although I'm often
tempted to switch things
up, this is a combination
I revisit over and over.
These tiny, crunchy gems
keep nearly forever in a
jar and are equally at
home alongside a glass of
prosecco or a macchiato.
I also like them crushed
into a little cup of creamy
vaniglia or melone gelato.
If I don't have cornmeal
on hand, I've substituted
corn flour and even masa
harina on occasion with
no problem. Use the most
fragrant rosemary and
freshest fennel seeds you
can find—it makes a
difference.*

MAKES 2½ DOZEN
BISCOTTINI

¾ cup | 3.5 oz | 100 g whole
   wheat pastry flour

½ cup | 2.5 oz | 70 g
   unbleached all-
   purpose flour

Scant ¼ cup | 0.75 oz | 20 g
   fine cornmeal

½ teaspoon non-aluminum
   baking powder

½ teaspoon fine-grain
   sea salt

Grated zest of 1 lemon

1 tablespoon chopped fresh
   rosemary

1 teaspoon fennel seeds

¼ cup | 2 oz | 60g unsalted
   butter, at room
   temperature

¾ cup | 3.5 oz | 100 g sifted
   natural brown sugar

2 eggs

2 teaspoons limoncello
   (optional)

¾ cup | 3.5 oz | 85 g whole
   almonds, toasted then
   chopped

Combine the flours, cornmeal, baking powder, salt, lemon zest, rosemary, and fennel seeds in a bowl; set aside. Use an electric mixer to cream the butter and sugar together until light and fluffy. Add one egg and the limoncello and mix until uniform. Add the dry ingredients to the wet and mix until the dough just comes together. Gently stir in the almonds by hand. Gather the dough into a ball, cut it in quarters, then refrigerate, covered, for 10 to 15 minutes.

Preheat the oven to 350°F | 180°C. Line a baking sheet with parchment paper. Whisk the remaining egg with the water to make a wash.

On a floured surface, roll each portion of dough into a 1-inch | 2.5cm wide tube. Carefully transfer to the baking sheet, flatten a bit, brush with the egg wash, then bake for 20 to 25 minutes, until golden. Remove from the oven and let cool. Transfer to a cutting board and use a serrated knife to cut ½-inch | 1.2cm thick slices. Arrange on the baking sheet and bake for another 10 to 15 minutes, or until golden. Allow to cool, then store in an airtight jar for up to 3 weeks.

Almond Cake

amaro * almond paste * eggs

Herbal, sweet, and bitter; some versions weak, others strong—not everyone loves amaro, the widely varied Italian digestif originally sold as a health tonic in the early nineteenth century. You still see bottles lining enoteca shelves. I love it, and often sip it straight, or over a cube or two of ice. It's invigorating like an alcoholic wheatgrass shot. On the culinary front, I use it for flavor, primarily in sweet preparations—sometimes with creams or granitas, and other times in baking: this cake, for example, where amaro's green herbaceousness melds beautifully with a thick almond paste batter, and glaze accent.

MAKES ONE 8-INCH | 20CM CAKE OR MULTIPLE SMALLER ONES

1½ cups | 14 oz | 400 g almond paste (see Notes, page 230)

5 large eggs, whisked

¼ cup | 1.75 oz | 50 g organic cornstarch

Scant ½ teaspoon fine-grain sea salt

5 tablespoons | 2.5 oz | 70 g unsalted butter, melted and cooled

3 tablespoons amaro

AMARO GLAZE

Scant 1 cup | 5 oz | 140 g organic confectioners' sugar

3 tablespoons plus 1 teaspoon amaro

Preheat the oven to 350°F | 180°C. Butter an 8-inch | 20cm pan, generously and evenly sprinkle with flour, and tap out any excess. (Alternatively, you can use multiple smaller pans for a cluster of tiny cakes; see Notes, page 230.)

Break the almond paste into a food processor and give a few quick pulses; you're looking for medium-size, pebbly pieces. Add the eggs and process until very smooth. Sprinkle in the cornstarch and salt and pulse a few times, then add the butter and amaro. Blend once more before transferring to the prepared pan(s). Bake until deeply golden and set in the center; you're going to want to test this cake—a toothpick should come out clean before pulling it from the oven—for tiny cakes, this is usually 40 to 45 minutes, longer for larger cakes. Let cool in the pan on a cooling rack for 20 to 30 minutes (very small cakes can be turned out after about 5 minutes), then transfer directly to the cooling rack. Let cool completely before glazing.

To make the glaze, whisk together the confectioners' sugar and amaro. Keep whisking until the glaze is free of lumps. Flood the top(s) of the cake(s), allowing the glaze to run over the sides. Alternatively, you can top each slice of cake with berries that have been tossed with a splash of amaro and sprinkled with brown sugar.

NOTES:

Be sure to buy almond paste, not marzipan. There is a difference.

This recipe makes about 3 cups | 710 ml of cake batter. You can bake one 8-inch | 20cm cake or multiple smaller ones. Adjust your baking time accordingly and use a cake tester to decide when to pull the cake(s) from the oven—smaller cakes take less time to bake.

Moka Pot Espresso

espresso coffee beans ✶ hot water

Although many in San Francisco have embraced pour-over
and Aeropress coffee brewing techniques, if you rent an
apartment in Italy, you'll likely find the ubiquitous Moka pot.
It's a classic 1930s-era coffee maker, and there has been one to
greet us in just about every apartment we've rented. They're
inexpensive little powerhouses that brew big-bodied, strong
extractions, often with a touch of crema. These are
pots of coffee that don't mess around.

For the best results, source good coffee, preferably an espresso
roast. Ideally, you'd grind the beans just before brewing, but
buying preground espresso is fine too. You want a medium
grind—not quite as fine as you'd use for a shot, not as coarse
as you'd use for a drip. Too fine, and you'll have a clogged pot.
If this happens, or you see the pressure release valve
popping out, start over with a coarser grind.

Pour hot water into the base, filling it to just shy of the
pressure valve. By using hot water to start, you prevent the
top chamber from overheating and scorching the coffee.

Fill the basket with ground coffee, then level it off.
The surface should be smooth; there's no need to pack
or tamp the grounds. Place the funnel into the base and
carefully screw the top chamber to the bottom. Tighten it with
conviction. If you thread it wrong or don't get a good
seal, you'll have a mess.

Place the pot on your stove over low heat for roughly
5 minutes while your coffee fills the top chamber. If it takes
longer, adjust the heat the next time. I tend to scale back the
heat when I hear it gurgle, or about halfway through. If you
forget, it's okay. Just be mindful that if the coffee gets too hot,
it will burn. When finished, remove from the heat and serve
immediately, either black or with a bit of sugar and cream.

FRANCE

Paris

PARIS IS TWO DOZEN CULTURED BUTTERS IN THE DAIRY CASE. It's sixteen different languages spoken in the crowded Métro car between Place de Clichy and Rochechouart. It's the best falafel of your life, buildings a thousand shades of cream, and brilliantly clean Mercedes-Benz taxicabs.

It's taking your morning coffee in a café gazing at thick molding fashioned into an ornate nasturtium motif, your reflection in a triptych expanse of pockmarked mirrors. It is where you can get impeccable quiche, crepes, tartines, fresh-pressed juice, microroasted coffee, futomaki, Champagne or sparkling sake, donburi, or tapas.

I do what it takes to get to Paris. Sometimes I stay in old hotels, sometimes new and hip ones. I've traded apartments with friends to visit for longer stretches, and on other occasions I've rented independently. Sometimes I have access to a kitchen to cook in, other times not. Like many, I unapologetically embrace being a tourist in Paris—more so than other cities—my heart full while shouldering up to mobs of travelers milling through Atelier Brancusi or reveling in Monet's *Nympheas* at L'Orangerie.

Hemingway wrote a series of dispatches from Paris for the *Toronto Daily Star* from 1920 to 1924, and I tend to think of a string of his sentences on approach to Charles de Gaulle Airport, just before landing, when we've descended over the English Channel and bank broadly around the perimeter of La Ville-Lumière: "There is a magic in the name France. It is a magic like the smell of the sea or the sight of blue hills or of soldiers marching by. It is a very old magic."

And that—along with so much else—is the draw of Paris. It's where you let a quiet *bar a vin* steal an entire afternoon, or happily surrender choice to the brusque proprietress at a bustling *fromagerie*. Or while walking from one point to another, you take a moment to sit on a bench in the Palais-Royale surrounded by a riot of colorful summer blooms.

My Paris Pantry

ALMONDS

BERRIES

CAPERS

CHERVIL

CHEESE

CHOCOLATE

CIDER

CITRUS

CRÈME FRAÎCHE

CROISSANTS

CULTURED BUTTER

CURRANTS

FARRO

FRESH SHELL BEANS

FROMAGE BLANC

GARLIC

HARICOTS VERTS

HAZELNUTS

HERBS

HONEY

KALE

LENTILS

LILLET

MUSHROOMS

MUSTARD

OLIVES

PAIN LEVAIN

PASTIS

PEARLED BARLEY

QUATRE ÉPICES

RADICCHIO

SAUTERNES

SORREL

TENDER LETTUCES

THYME

TOMATO

WINE VINEGAR

RENSEIGNEMENTS : • TEL : 01.43.26.46.47   http://guignolduluxembourg.monsite.or

DIMANCHE 11H   15ʰ.15.   16ʰ.30.   PINOCCHIO

LUNDI FERME

MARDI FERME

MERCREDI   15ʰ.15.   16ʰ.30.   •LES 3 PETITS COCH

JEUDI FERME

VENDREDI FERME

SAMEDI A 11H. *les 3 petits cochons* 15ʰ.15.   16ʰ.30.   PINOCC

ON : FRANCIS–CLAUDE DESARTHIS • 86.RUE NOTRE–DAME DES CHAMPS 7500

Lucques in Grapefruit Juice

green olives * grapefruit juice * olive oil

You see a lot of Moroccan and Spanish citrus in Parisian street markets, neighboring olive sellers and cheesemongers. And this is one of my favorite ways to do something extra special with the gorgeous French olive varietals and put citrus to use at the same time. Olives are slit, arranged to soak in freshly squeezed grapefruit juice, and topped with a good amount of olive oil. The citrus permeates the olives, making them an easy, special appetizer always at the ready in your refrigerator. Of the French olives, Lucques work particularly well, but picholines will also do. Plump, buttery, Italian Castelvetranos are my olive of choice when I make these at home. They're great served along with Vin de Pamplemousse (page 264) and good bread for dunking in the citrus-bolstered olive oil.

MAKES 2 CUPS

12 oz | 340 g green olives, drained

1 cup | 240 ml freshly squeezed grapefruit juice

A few tablespoons of extra-virgin olive oil

Tiny cheese cubes and chopped herbs, to serve (optional)

Slit each of your olives 2 or 3 times with a sharp paring knife and arrange, compactly, in a clean jar. Cover the olives with grapefruit juice and finish with at least ½ inch | 1.2 cm of olive oil. The olives will keep like this, refrigerated, for months.

Serve the olives, drained, at room temperature along with some of the olive oil. Alternatively, preheat the oven to 350°F | 175°C and place the olives in a shallow baking dish, along with tiny cubes of cheese, a showering of herbs, and a generous drizzle of olive oil. Bake until the olives are hot throughout and their skins start to pucker a bit.

Baby Artichoke Salad

lemon cucumber ✳ melted leek ✳ new potatoes

This is an artichoke-centric take on French potato salad. It's particularly good in the spring, when new potatoes, artichokes, and leeks are in season and at their most tender. But this salad can be a good option any time of year by trading out the artichokes for whatever is vibrant and seasonal at the market: broccoli, green beans, and raddichio are all good options.

SERVES 4

8 small new potatoes

8 baby artichokes

Freshly squeezed lemon juice

4 tablespoons | 60 ml extra-virgin olive oil

1 medium clove garlic, smashed

Fine-grain sea salt

¼ cup | 60 ml water

2 cups | 8 oz | 225 g very thinly sliced leeks, well washed

1 tablespoon white wine vinegar

2 small lemon cucumbers, seeded, cut into ¼-inch | 6mm thick crescents

Fennel or dill fronds or fresh herbs, to finish

Place the potatoes in a saucepan, cover with well-salted water, and set over medium-high heat until the water is boiling. Boil the potatoes until tender, but not falling apart, about 10 minutes. Drain, cut them into wedges, and set aside.

In the meantime, pull all the tough outer leaves from the artichokes and keep going until you reach the tender inner leaves. Trim off the stem and ½ inch | 1.2 cm or so of the top. Use a paring knife to trim around the base, removing any rough remains of leaves. Slice in half lengthwise and place in a bowl of water with lemon juice added until ready to use, to keep the artichokes from browning. If there is any fuzziness inside the artichokes, carve it out with a spoon.

Heat 1 tablespoon of the olive oil in a skillet over medium heat. Add the garlic, the prepared artichokes, a scant ½ teaspoon of salt, and the water. Toss to coat. Cook, covered, for 5 minutes. Then remove the cover and continue to cook, tossing regularly, until the water has evaporated and the artichokes are tender, 3 to 5 minutes. Remove from the pan and set aside.

In the same pan, over medium-low heat, add the remaining 3 tablespoons olive oil, the leeks, and another scant

½ teaspoon of salt. Stir regularly, avoiding any browning on the leeks. When they're wilted, after 4 to 6 minutes, stir in the vinegar and continue to cook on low for another 8 minutes, until completely silky and tender. Take off the heat and let cool just until warm.

Just before serving, combine the potatoes, artichokes, leeks, and cucumbers in a bowl or platter, then drizzle with about 2 tablespoons of lemon juice, and adjust seasoning to taste. Finish with fennel or dill fronds or fresh herbs.

Wine-Washed Arugula

toasted croissants ✳ Chablis ✳ chèvre

*My eyes are often bigger
than my appetite when
I queue up at Du Pain
et des Idées, the much
celebrated bakery in the
Tenth Arrondissement. It
uses organic flours and
offers a gorgeous daily
arrangement including*
pain des amis, pain au
chocolat, *and* chaussons.
*That said, I love a classic
croissant. Plain. And I
have a tendency to buy too
many. I've taken to toasting
shards of the day-old
leftovers into croutons of
sorts and tossing them in
simple salads like this one.
Make it with a good splash
of whatever wine is open—
preferably a good, crisp,
dry white.*

SERVES 4

A bowl of arugula

A few glugs of olive oil

A generous splash of dry,
crisp white wine (for
example, Chablis)

Fine-grain sea salt

Torn herbs

Day-old croissants, torn
and well toasted

Chunks of chèvre

Just before sitting down to eat, toss the arugula with
olive oil, wine, salt to taste, and whatever fresh herbs
you have on hand. Finish with the croissant pieces and
a bit of chèvre.

Tartines

Paris celebrates a culture of tartines—open-faced sandwiches
served on toasted slabs of rustic levain bread. It's what
I eat most days there, as part of a formula lunch—tartine plus
salad plus glass of wine or water. Here is the first of three
riffs inspired by the general concept.

Tartine aux Endives

apricot ✳ marjoram ✳ sheep's milk cheese

SERVES 4

2 tablespoons extra-virgin olive oil, plus more for serving

4 (½-inch | 1.2cm thick) slices levain bread

3 endives, cored and sliced into ¼-inch | 6mm ribbons (about 2 cups)

½ teaspoon fine-grain sea salt

2 teaspoons freshly squeezed lemon juice

2 ripe fresh apricots or dried apricots, thinly sliced

¼ cup | 1.5 oz | 45 g toasted and sliced pecans

⅓ cup | 2 oz | 60 g crumbled or shaved, hard sheep's milk cheese (Manchego, pecorino, Pyrenees)

2 teaspoons fresh marjoram leaves

Lightly oil each slice of bread and toast or broil until golden and crisp. A few minutes before serving, place the endives into a bowl with the salt and lemon juice. Let it sit for a few minutes, until the endives wilt a bit. Add the apricots, pecans, and cheese and toss. To assemble, evenly distribute the endive mixture across the bread, then finish with fresh marjoram and a drizzle of olive oil.

(continued)

Tartine au Fromage Blanc

saffron onions * cherries * watercress

SERVES 4

2 tablespoons butter

10 saffron threads

½ teaspoon fine-grain
sea salt

1 medium onion, halved
and thinly sliced

1 tablespoon good white
wine vinegar

2½ cups | 12.5 oz | 355 g
pitted and halved sweet
cherries (optional)

A few tablespoons of extra-
virgin olive oil

4 (¾-inch | 2cm thick)
slices levain bread

¾ cup | 3 oz | 85 g
fromage blanc

Pea shoots, watercress,
or arugula, to finish

In a pot, melt the butter over low heat. Crush the saffron with the salt in a mortar and pestle and add to the pot. Stir in the onion and vinegar and continue to cook until the onion is soft and silky, 10 minutes or so. Patience is key here, and you should avoid browning the onions or butter. At this point, add the cherries and cook for an additional 8 to 10 minutes. The cherries should soften but still retain their shape and structure. Remove from heat and set aside; you can make this component a day or two ahead of time, bringing to room temperature before using. (It should also be noted that when cherries aren't in season, simply omit them.)

Lightly oil the bread and toast or broil until golden and crisp. To assemble, spread 3 tablespoons of fromage blanc on each slice of bread. Spoon a generous portion of the cherry/onion mixture with its juice onto the fromage blanc and drizzle with olive oil. Garnish with tangles of watercress or pea shoots, or if those are not available, arugula is a fine substitute.

Tartine au Fleur de Courge

avocado ⁎ coconut oil ⁎ macadamia nuts

SERVES 4

¾ cup | 3 oz | 85 g finely chopped toasted macadamia nuts

1 small clove garlic, finely grated

Zest of 1 medium orange

4 squash blossoms or basil, sliced in chiffonade

4 green onions, thinly sliced

Scant ½ teaspoon fine-grain sea salt

4 (¾-inch | 2cm thick) slices levain bread

¼ cup | 60 ml extra-virgin coconut oil

2 small, ripe avocados, halved and pitted

Extra virgin olive oil, for serving

Combine the macadamia nuts, garlic, orange zest, squash blossoms, green onions, and salt in a small bowl and mix thoroughly. Toast or broil the bread until it's golden and crisp. Just before serving, while the bread is still warm, place 1 tablespoon of the coconut oil on each *tartine* and evenly spread, saturating the toast. Spoon half of an avocado onto each piece of toast and smash it, then distribute the nut mixture equally over the *tartines*. Finish with a drizzle of olive oil and season to your liking.

Gougères

whole wheat * Comté * soft herbs

Golden pom-poms of cheese and herb-flecked magic, gougères are pure delight. I'm all about keeping the process as simple as possible, opting for a one-pan method and stirring the batter by hand, not bothering with a mixer. Instead of fussing with a pastry bag, I push dollops of the dough onto parchment lined baking sheets from a spoon. A couple of tips: Be sure to use large eggs, not extra-large, and prep all your ingredients ahead of time. Related to baking, be sure the gougères brown all the way, particularly up the sides, before pulling them from the oven. The resulting structure will prevent the tops from caving in.

MAKES ABOUT 2 DOZEN
3-INCH | 7.5CM GOUGÈRES

⅔ cup | 160 ml water

⅓ cup | 80 ml milk

½ cup | 4 oz | 115 ml butter, thickly sliced

¾ teaspoon fine-grain sea salt

Scant ½ cup | 2.25 oz | 65 g all-purpose flour

Scant ½ cup | 2.25 oz | 65 g whole wheat flour

4 eggs, at room temperature

1¼ cups | 3.25 oz | 90 g grated Comté, Gruyère, or Cantal

4 tablespoons finely chopped soft herbs (see Note)

Preheat the oven to 425°F | 220°C, with racks placed in the top and bottom thirds. Line two baking sheets with parchment paper.

In a large heavy saucepan over medium-high heat, bring the water, milk, butter, and salt just to a boil, then dial back the heat a bit. Add the flours and stir with a wooden spoon—really go at it—for a couple of minutes, until the dough comes together smoothly, is glossy, and gives off a faint toasted scent. Remove from the heat and let cool for about 5 minutes—long enough that the eggs won't cook when you work them in.

One at a time, add each of the four eggs, stirring vigorously after each addition. Stir in 1 cup | 2.5 oz | 72 g of the cheese and the herbs. Right away, scoop the gougères onto the prepared baking sheets in heaping tablespoon-size dollops, leaving at least 1½ inches | 4 cm between each. Sprinkle with the remaining cheese.

Place in the oven, bake for 5 minutes, then dial the heat back to 375°F | 190°C and bake for another 20 to 25 minutes, or until the gougères are deeply golden all over, puffed, and well set. If you notice the gougères in the back browning much more quickly than the ones in the front, spin the sheet 180 degrees about two-thirds of the way through without letting much heat out of the oven—be quick.

Alternately, if you aren't baking the gougères immediately: shape pans of gougère dough, sprinkle with cheese, and freeze for half an hour. Transfer to a well-sealed freezer bag until you're ready to bake. Bake straight from the freezer, as above; they may need a couple extra minutes.

NOTE: Try these herb combinations: 1 tablespoon each of fresh thyme, tarragon, oregano, and dill; or, 1 tablespoon each of fresh chives, tarragon, chervil, and thyme.

Lettuce Hearts with Melted Butter

garlic * salt * lemon

At least once each trip, I make a point to seek out the most tender lettuces I can find in Paris in order to make this Elizabeth David salad. It was published in French Country Cooking *(1951) and will likely have you thinking of lettuce more as a vegetable than as a salad green by the time you're done.*

She tells us, "Use only the tenderest of lettuce hearts for this exquisite salad; arrange them in a salad bowl, season them very lightly with salt and a scrape of sugar, and at the last moment pour over them warm melted butter into which you have pounded a very small piece of garlic and a squeeze of lemon."

For those of you who are more comfortable with exact measurements, I typically use 5 or 6 tiny heads of Baby Gem or baby romaine lettuce, ⅓ cup | 2.75 oz | 75 g of melted butter, a garlic clove, and a scant tablespoon of lemon juice. Feel free to toss in chopped herbs, a bit of grated cheese, and/or some toasted nuts if you're inclined to fancy it up a bit. Another twist on the general idea is to let the butter brown.

SERVES 4

Madeleines

millet * brown butter

*I spend a lot of time
combing Paris flea markets
for old pans, bakeware,
tart tins, and interesting
cutlery. Over the years,
I've come across a number
of beautiful madeleine
tins. One of the best has
impressions for the tiniest
of madeleines; my other
favorite has a seashell
motif. These charming
little cakes bake up golden
and tender in the decades-
old pans. I started baking
madeleines years ago, using
Dorie Greenspan's recipe
(before I was lucky enough
to call Dorie a friend)
because of an endorsement
from my friend Lanha
Hong-Porretta, the most
enthusiastic madeleine
baker I know. The recipe
has evolved quite a bit in
the years since, and here's
where it stands now.*

MAKES 2 TO 3 DOZEN
REGULAR MADELEINES

¾ cup | 6 oz | 180 g
  unsalted butter plus
  2 tablespoons softened
  unsalted butter for
  greasing the pan

¾ cups | 3.75 oz | 105 g
  whole wheat pastry flour,
  plus more for dusting
  the pan

4 eggs

¼ teaspoon fine-grain
  sea salt

⅔ cup | 2.75 oz | 80 g
  muscovado or natural
  brown sugar

3 tablespoons raw millet

Preheat the oven to 350°F | 175°F. Melt the ¾ cup of butter in a small pot over medium heat until it's brown and gives off a deliciously nutty aroma, roughly 20 minutes. Strain using a fine strainer or double layer of cheesecloth—you want to leave the solids behind. Cool the butter to room temperature.

While the browned butter is cooling, use the remaining 2 tablespoons butter to grease the madeleine molds—make sure you get into all the ridges in the molds. Dust the buttered molds with flour, then invert the pan and tap out any excess flour.

Put the eggs with the salt in the bowl of an electric mixer with a whisk attachment. Whip on high speed until thick—you are looking for the eggs to roughly double or triple in volume—approximately 3 minutes. Continue to mix on high speed, sprinkling the sugar in in two additions. Whip for 2 minutes or until the mixture is thick and ribbony. Sprinkle the flour on top of the egg batter and gently fold it in. Now fold in the browned butter, only stirring enough to bring everything together. Pour the batter into the molds, filling each mold two-thirds to three-quarters full, and sprinkle with millet. Bake the madeleines for 12 to 14 minutes (7 to 10 minutes for smaller cookies), or until the edges are golden brown. Remove from oven and unmold immediately. Cool on racks.

Vin Berries

wine ∗ berries

Fraises des bois are one of the elusive jewels of the fruit world—small, fragrant strawberries similar in scale to raspberries. I've encountered them a handful of times and only very recently at the San Francisco market I frequent. But in Paris (and Italy as well) they're more common. They're perfect for a preparation like this, but any small, ripe, sweet strawberries will do. Serve vin berries on their own or with a generous dollop of rose-spiked Sabayon (page 263) on top.

SERVES 2 TO 4

1 basket ripe strawberries
(about 12 oz | 340 g)

1 tablespoon maple syrup
or honey

⅔ cup | 160 ml cold
rosé wine

½ teaspoon fresh
thyme leaves

Use a wet cloth to gently brush away any dust or debris before using a paring knife to hull each berry, Slice into quarters and place in a shallow serving bowl. Drizzle with maple syrup and toss very gently; you'll want use more or less syrup depending on the sweetness of your berries. Pour in the wine and set aside for at least 10 or 15 minutes, tossing once or twice. Spoon into small cups using a slotted spoon and serve sprinkled with thyme.

Lillet Shrub

white wine vinegar ✳ frozen cherries ✳ Byrrh

Beyond Lillet, which is easy enough to come by, this summer shrub takes a splash of Byrrh. A bit more obscure, particularly here in the United States, it is a French apéritif made of red wine macerated with quinquina, coffee, bitter orange, and cocoa and matured in oak casks. It brings knockout color to a drink as well as a pronounced tonic-quinine flavor. Seek it out; the Lillet base and white wine vinegar backbone are also tasty without the Byrrh accent.

SERVES 2

¾ cup | 180 ml Lillet

1 tablespoon Byrrh

1 tablespoon good white wine (Sauvignon Blanc or Champagne) vinegar

Ice cubes

2 to 4 tablespoons soda water

Frozen cherries, to serve (optional)

Place a handful of ice cubes into a cocktail shaker (or Mason jar) along with the Lillet, Byrrh, and vinegar. Shake vigorously and strain into glasses filled with ice. Top with splashes of soda water and finish with something fresh, fruity, and pretty—frozen cherries are particularly nice.

Sabayon

Sauternes * cream * eggs

Correct or not, I think of sabayon as an alternative to chocolate mousse—one with no raw eggs. It can easily be tweaked many different ways depending on what else is being served and what sort of boozy accent you have on hand.

Sauternes is a classic option, but dry French cider, vin santo, or Lillet are all options. Fold leftover day-old, chopped meringues in for a real treat or torn and toasted leftover madeleine crumbs (see page 256).

SERVES 6

2 cups | 480 ml water

4 egg yolks

3 tablespoons natural cane sugar

Scant ¼ teaspoon fine-grain sea salt

Zest of ½ lemon, finely chopped

Scant ½ cup | 100 ml plus 2 tablespoons Sauternes

1 cup | 240 ml heavy whipping cream

Place the water in a saucepan over medium heat and bring to a simmer. In the meantime, whisk the egg yolks, sugar, and salt together in a stainless steel bowl until just combined. Whisk in the lemon zest and scant ½ cup | 100 ml of Sauternes and set the bowl over the simmering pot—be sure the bottom of the bowl is not touching the water. Whisk constantly until the mixture thickens into a rich, puddinglike custard.

Cover and refrigerate until cooled. Whip the heavy cream to the point it can hold big floppy peaks, add the remaining 2 tablespoons Sauternes, and beat a bit more. Spoon the chilled sabayon mixture over the whipped cream and gently fold together until uniform in color. Serve in small individual glasses or as a side to a tart or a fruit or cookie plate.

Vin de Pamplemousse

rosé wine * winter citrus

Although it takes a bit of planning and time, this is the definition of charm in a glass. People who love vin de pamplemousse *know it's the sort of thing to brew in the winter, when citrus is best, for enjoyment in warmer summer months. This blushing version of* vin de pamplemousse *takes a month and some to complete, but the resulting aperitif is pink, light, and lovely, particularly in a Picardie glass filled with ice—well worth the effort and the wait. I stock up on vanilla beans from the grand cru vanilla bar at Eric Roellinger on Rue Sainte-Anne just for this recipe.*

MAKES ABOUT FOUR
750ML BOTTLES

2 blood oranges

1 Cara Cara orange

2 lemons

3 Ruby Red grapefruits

½ vanilla bean

1½ cups | 7.5 oz | 210 g natural cane sugar

3½ (750ml) bottles rosé wine

2 cups | 480 ml vodka

Sanitize a 5-quart | 4.75L jar (see Note) and place it near your cutting board. Scrub the citrus well and slice it thinly—¼ inch | 6 mm or thinner. Place the slices in the jar along with the vanilla bean and sugar. Add the wine and then the vodka. You may need add a bit more wine because you want the fruit to be submerged with as little airspace at the top of the jar as possible. Seal tightly, then turn the jar upside down a few times to disperse the sugar. Store in a cool, dark place for approximately 40 days—a closet or basement works well.

Jostle and turn the *vin de pamplemousse* upside-down every day for the first week to help the sugar dissolve and extract the oils from the citrus peel. Then scale back, agitating the jar every 3 days.

After the 40 days, or when you're ready to bottle, sanitize 4 (750ml) bottles (or enough smaller size bottles to hold the mixture) and dry them well. Allow the glass to cool completely before filling. Strain the *vin de pamplemousse* into a sanitized bowl or other container; discard the citrus and vanilla. Fill the sanitized bottles, leaving an inch or so of headspace, and seal with caps or boiled corks. Transfer to the refrigerator and drink over the coming months or hold off until warmer weather. Serve over ice in small glasses.

NOTE: To sanitize the jars, bottles, and utensils for *vin de pamplemousse*, place clean glass jars and bottles, along with the utensils (make sure they are ovenproof), in a cold oven. Heat to 250°F | 120°C, and hold at this temperature for 30 minutes. Turn off the oven, open the oven door, and allow the items to cool before removing. Be mindful of keeping everything clean as you remove it from the oven, making sure the sanitized items come in contact only with clean surfaces.

INDIA

*New Delhi * Jaipur * Jodhpur * Agra * Nimaj*

EVEN THE MOST VIBRANT GREEN TREES and pink blossoms in New Delhi appear to be coated with a powder-fine dust. The result is a world of intense color dialed back by haze and dirt, dust and age. Shine is lost, garishness softened.

I spent nearly a month in the back of a small white Nissan driving around New Delhi and the cities of Rajasthan, in the expansive northern and western parts of the country. Our driver was named Shankar, and although we shared not more than ten words of common language, we did manage to get around pretty well. There was much pointing, confusion, circling—and, more often than not, success.

Wayne and I ate breakfasts of masala dosa, *idlii*, and *paratha*. We tried ice cream infused with crushed betel leaves and rose petals. There were sweet and salty lime sodas, triple strong ginger ales, *tawa* (fenugreek) paneer, long thali lunches, feisty tin bowls of *rasam*, and cold Kingfisher lagers best enjoyed at the height of afternoon heat. In the mornings, men were often crouched at the end of driveways sipping tea. There were women in bright saris sweeping before sunrise. We drove most days, often long distances, past fields of golden marigold, then millet, henna, wheat, and cotton. We navigated the barrage of Rajasthani transport lorries, goatherds, motor bikes, rickshaws, camel carts, and shin-deep potholes.

In the intense Agra heat, we sat for a while behind the Taj Mahal alongside many families. The shade cast by the monument kept the marble cool, and a generous breeze swept across the scene as sandal-footed aunties

267

and cousins and elders snapped photos, or strolled, or simply stretched out and rested, gazing at the Yamuna River as the sun made its crawl to the horizon.

My India Pantry

BLACK PEPPER

CARDAMOM

CHICKPEAS

CHILES

CINNAMON

CORIANDER

CUMIN

CURRY LEAVES

FENUGREEK

GARAM MASALA

GHEE

GINGER

GREENS

LEMON

LENTILS

LIME

MILLET

MUSTARD

PANEER

ROSE

SAFFRON

SESAME

TURMERIC

YOGURT

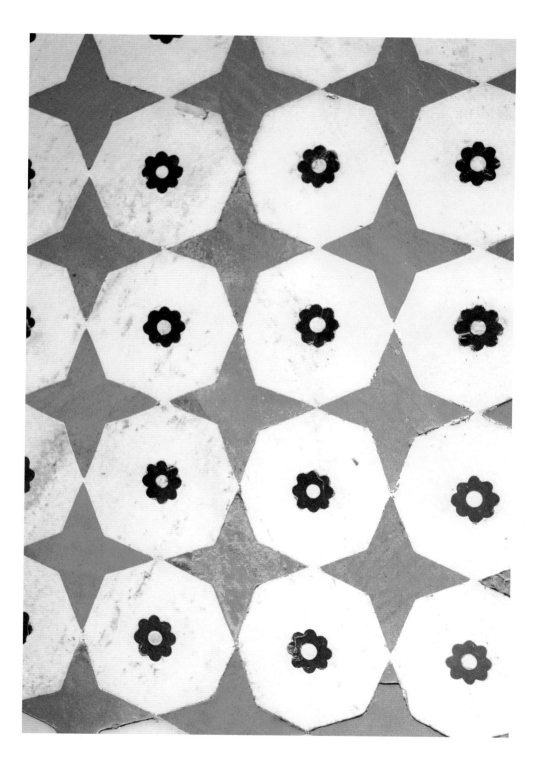

Vaghareli Makai

corn * peanuts * cilantro *
mustard seeds * sesame seeds

*Flying into Delhi in the middle of the night is disorienting.
We arrived at our hotel only after weaving through freeways,
on-ramps and off-ramps, and darkened tree-lined side streets,
eventually resting our heads after 2 a.m. The morning brought
masala dosa and lassi for breakfast, and we decided to dive
into Old Delhi's chaotic Chandni Chowk straight away—a sea
of people, rickshaws, and sidewalk rubble, and an assault of
signage. We sought out feathery layered and stuffed parathas
for lunch at a stall where you sit on a bench facing the narrow,
ancient alleyways before you. And after, we made our way to
the spice market, where I saw a cluster of women in electric
green and pink saris crouched in a strip of dirt between
spice vendors. They were sorting pistachios—nut from shell.
One was eating a simple bowl of rice topped with a smear
of what looked like an Indian harissa paste and edged by a
peanut-corn vegetable medley of sorts. It was beautiful and
simple and you knew at a glance it tasted good. Here's my
version. You can enjoy it over rice, over lentils, or on its own
as a side dish. It's best with fresh corn—although you can use
frozen corn that has thawed. Even better, swap in chopped
asparagus, broccoli, or another vegetable when
corn isn't in season.*

(Pictured on page 278.)

2 small fresh red chile peppers, stemmed

2 medium cloves garlic

1 (1-inch | 2.5cm) piece of ginger

¼ teaspoon turmeric

¾ teaspoon fine-grain sea salt

2 tablespoons clarified butter (see page 315), ghee (page 314), or sunflower oil

1½ teaspoons yellow or brown mustard seeds

1 pound | 455 g fresh corn kernels

½ cup | 2 oz | 55 g roasted peanuts

1 cup | 1 oz | 30 g chopped cilantro

1 or 2 lemons, cut into wedges and seeded

2 tablespoons toasted sesame seeds

Use a mortar and pestle or a food processor to smash the chiles, garlic, ginger, turmeric, and salt into a paste. Heat the butter in a skillet over medium-high heat. Add the mustard seeds, and once they have begun to pop, stir in the corn. Cook, stirring gently but constantly for a minute or so, then add the peanuts, half of the cilantro, and half of the prepared chile paste. Cook for another minute or so; taste, and add the rest of the paste if you don't find the dish too spicy, and a good squeeze or two of lemon juice. Taste and adjust the seasoning if needed.

Serve topped with the remaining cilantro, the sesame seeds, and the remaining lemon wedges.

Vaghareli Makai (page 276)

Saag Paneer (page 280), Paratha (page 299), Aloo Bhaji (page 285)

Saag Paneer

garam masala ∗ chile flakes ∗ garlic

In the shadow of Jodhpur's clock tower, there is a small, family spice shop run by sisters. It opens wide to a theater of people hustling here and there, open-air trading, buses, wandering cows, and dust. There are seven sisters in total, and they've had a tough, but ultimately successful, go of things after inheriting the spice business following the sudden death of their father a decade ago. Female spice traders are exceptionally rare in Jodhpur, and building on their father's legacy of quality and knowledge, Mohanlal Verhomal Spices (or MV Spices for short) is an inspiration to female entrepreneurs in India or otherwise. I packed a substantial range of their blends in my suitcase for the return home, and the garam masala became a staple in what I consider my lazy, weeknight saag paneer.

Instead of hand-chopping the copious amounts of spinach needed in a preparation like this, I use a hand blender to cream the spinach, and then reintroduce a bit of texture with minced onions. It's a simple way to get a jolt of greens all in one go, and leftovers are great on Paratha (page 299) or other flatbread, swirled into eggs, or folded into lentils for a one-bowl meal. Using baby spinach saves time as well, because you don't need to stem the spinach. I also like to do a version with stemmed mustard greens—or any combination of greens, really. Nettles are a great addition when they're in season as well.

(Pictured on page 279.)

MAKES ABOUT 3 CUPS

3 tablespoons sunflower oil or ghee (page 314)

1½ pounds | 680 g baby spinach, well washed

1 teaspoon whole cumin seeds

1 teaspoon fine-grain sea salt

1 scant teaspoon red chile flakes

4 medium cloves garlic, smashed

2 small white onions, minced

2 teaspoons garam masala

⅓ cup | 80 ml buttermilk

Lots of fresh lemon juice

6 oz | 170 g Fresh Paneer (page 292)

Chives or chive blossoms, to serve (optional)

Place 1 tablespoon of the oil in a large pot over medium-high heat. When hot, add the spinach and stir until it begins to collapse. You may need to add it in two or three additions, but get all the spinach in the pot as quickly as you can. Once it has collapsed, but is still bright, a couple of minutes, remove from heat, drain, and blend to a puree with a hand blender. Set aside.

Give the pot you cooked the spinach in a quick rinse, and then place it over medium-high heat with the remaining 2 tablespoons of oil. Add the cumin seeds, salt, red pepper flakes, garlic, and onions. Cook until the onion is translucent, a couple of minutes. Stir in the garam masala, dial back the heat, and stir in the spinach. Gradually stir in the buttermilk and bring to a simmer. Stir in a couple of big squeezes of lemon juice. Taste and adjust the seasoning, fold in the paneer (or sprinkle it on top), and finish with a sprinkling of chives or chive blossoms.

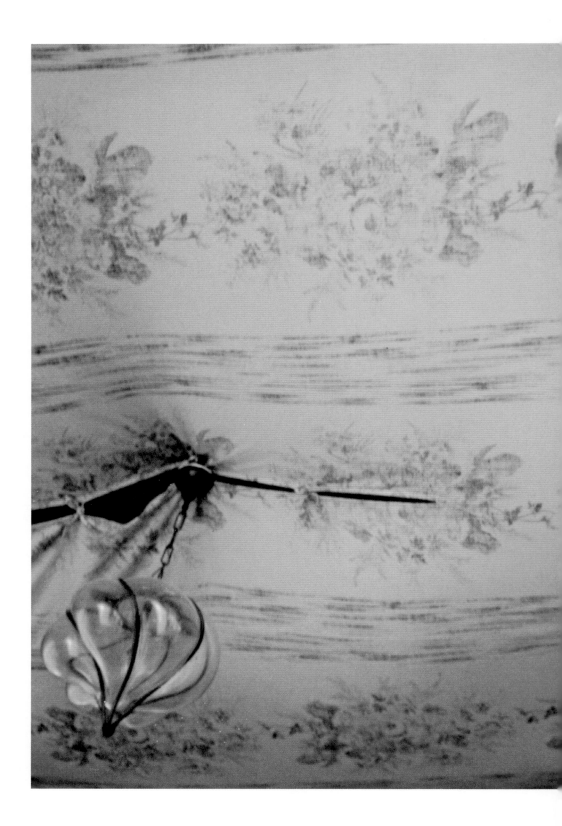

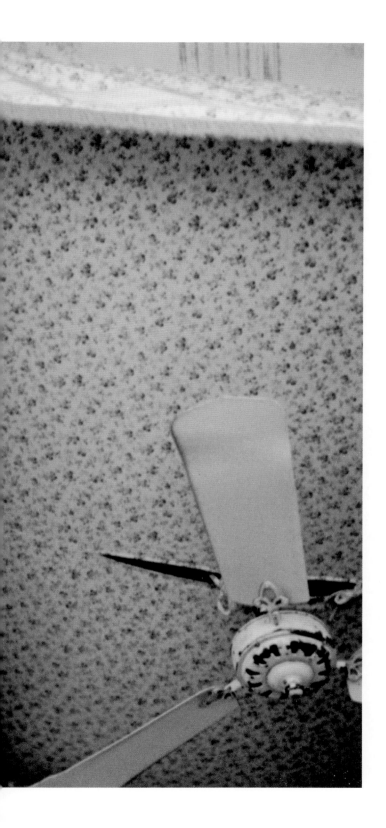

Aloo Bhaji

green chiles * fenugreek * sesame * cumin

Nutty and piquant, with hints of burnt sugar, the combination of sesame, green chile, and fenugreek I encountered a number of times in Rajasthan was a fragrant revelation. Use it here with the best little new potatoes you can find. Potatoes are parboiled until tender, a step you can take a day or more ahead of time. After roasting in a hot oven until crisp and brown, the insides remain fluffy, hot, and delicate. Go as far as you dare to go in regards to roasting: the skins will crisp, while the spices perfume the kitchen. You can do an alternative version with cauliflower in place of the potatoes.

SERVES 4 TO 6

1 pound | 450 g small
   new potatoes

7 tablespoons clarified
   butter (see page 315)

1½ teaspoons cumin

2 serrano chiles, seeded
   and minced

1½ teaspoons whole yellow
   mustard seed

½ teaspoon ground
   fenugreek

8 small shallots

2 whole heads garlic,
   top third cut off

Fine-grain sea salt

3 tablespoons toasted
   sesame seeds

Preheat the oven to 375°F | 180°C. Give the potatoes a good scrub and place them in a large pot of boiling salted water. Simmer until just tender, about 10 minutes. Drain well and set aside.

In a large cast-iron or ovenproof skillet or casserole, melt the butter over medium heat, and when hot, stir in the cumin, most of the serrano chiles, and the mustard and fenugreek. Sauté until fragrant, barely a minute, and carefully add the potatoes to the skillet, in a single layer if possible. Toss gently to coat with butter and spices and remove from the heat. Nestle the shallots and garlic alongside the potatoes, sprinkle with ½ teaspoon of salt, and move to the oven. Roast for 60 minutes, tossing once or twice along the way, until the potatoes are deeply golden and the garlic and shallots are perfectly soft. Serve sprinkled generously with the sesame seeds and the remaining serrano chiles.

Mustard Seed Oil Fried Eggs

cumin * kale * avocado

Cold-pressed mustard seed oil is spicy and worth seeking out. It mellows in the pan, but a finishing drizzle across the eggs here brings the flavor right back to the forefront. You're also getting mustard flavor from mustard seeds, so if you don't have mustard seed oil, trade it for extra-virgin coconut oil or clarified butter.

SERVES 4

2 teaspoons cold-pressed mustard seed oil, plus more for serving

4 eggs

12 lacinato kale leaves, stemmed and sliced into ribbons

2 tablespoons raw sunflower seeds

Fine-grain sea salt

½ teaspoon yellow mustard seeds

½ teaspoon cumin seeds

¼ cup | 0.5 oz | 15 g grated Gruyère cheese

Salted plain yogurt, for serving

Chopped avocado, for serving

Heat a large cast-iron skillet over medium heat. Once hot, add the mustard seed oil. Carefully crack the eggs into the skillet and cook, covered, until the whites set and the yolks are to your liking. If your skillet isn't large enough, you may need to cook the eggs two at a time. Transfer the eggs to a plate. Add the kale, sunflower seeds, and a pinch of salt to the empty skillet and increase the heat to medium-high. You want the seeds to toast a bit, but not burn. When your kale is just about cooked and the sunflower seeds are toasted, stir in the mustard seeds and cumin for the final moments. Remove from the heat and stir in the cheese.

Serve each fried egg with a bit of kale, a dollop of salted yogurt, some avocado, and the smallest drizzle of mustard seed oil.

Rasam

black pepper * chana dal * lime

A good rasam *is a thing of beauty—strong, restorative, invigorating. And while* rasams *are heartily spiced soups typical of South Indian cuisine, I encountered inspired versions throughout Delhi and Rajasthan. This version is not shy—built around a brothy mainline of black pepper and set off by a strong chorus of ginger, chile, and lime, it commands attention. The cumin and mustard bring an earthiness, the cilantro a fresh, bright, and green finish.*

SERVES 6

1 cup | 7 oz | 200 g chana dal or yellow split peas

1½ teaspoons whole cumin seeds

1½ teaspoons whole black peppercorns

2 tablespoons ghee (page 314) or clarified butter (see page 315)

1 tablespoon black mustard seeds

1½ tablespoons seeded and finely minced serrano chile (about 1 large)

2 tablespoons finely minced peeled fresh ginger

3 medium cloves garlic, finely minced

1 small onion, minced

1 tablespoon ground turmeric

1 (28-oz | 795g) can crushed tomatoes

2 teaspoons fine-grain sea salt

4 cups | 1 L water

1 small lime, scrubbed and cut in half

1 cup | 1 oz | 30 g finely chopped cilantro

Place the dal in a bowl, cover with at least an inch | 2.5 cm of water, and allow to soak for 30 minutes. Drain before using.

Make the spice blend by placing the cumin seeds and peppercorns in a dry pan over medium heat; toast until fragrant. The cumin will darken a bit—be mindful to toast, not burn it. Transfer to a mortar and pestle or spice mill, and grind into a fine powder.

In a large pot over medium-high heat, melt the ghee. When hot, add the black mustard seeds, swirling the pan so the seeds cover the bottom; cover with a lid. The seeds will start to pop—avoid lifting the lid while this is happening. When the popping quiets down, after a minute or so, stir in the chile, ginger, garlic, and onion. Sauté until everything is fragrant and the onions have softened and become slightly translucent, 4 to 5 minutes. Stir in the chana dal and turmeric and toss to coat. Add the tomatoes, cumin-pepper spice blend, salt, and water. Squeeze the lime halves into the pot, mindful to omit any seeds, and place the spent lime halves into the pot as well. Dial down the heat to medium and simmer for 20 to 30 minutes, just until the dal is soft and tender. Before serving, discard the lime halves, add the cilantro, and bring back to a simmer. Thin with more water if needed, adjust the seasoning, remove from the heat, and serve.

Fresh Paneer

whole milk ∗ lemon juice ∗ salt

*A few months after returning home from India, I received a
package from Jaipur. My name was in thick black marker,
and the box itself was wrapped in fabric, stitched crudely,
tight at the seams. Inside was a treasure of culinary treats
from Melissa Millward. She runs Anokhi Café in Rajasthan's
pink city, and I was fortunate to spend time with her on the
Anokhi Farm. Melissa sent me a number of treats, including
gur and gur shakkar (raw Indian sugars), as well as a
plastic strainer, which, as she noted, "is perfect for straining
yogurt or paneer without the messy hassle of a muslin bag."
She also noted it was actually a water strainer: "Scary, but
true." The strainer is flimsy plastic and hard on the eyes,
and while I typically avoid plastic, it's effective.*

*If you've ever made homemade ricotta, you'll understand how
simple it is to make fresh paneer. The reasons to do so are
compelling: homemade paneer is bright, with a nice curd; you
can keep it as light as you want, or press it into a more solid
form; store-bought paneer is often flavorless and rubbery. Use
good whole milk, and—although I typically make my paneer
plain—there is no reason you can't add spices, lemon zest, or
black pepper at the same time you add the salt. One trick I've
learned is to rig my strainer atop a tall vessel, so the cheese
sits high above the whey as it drains. Flower vases
tend to be the best candidates in my kitchen.*

MAKES ABOUT
2½ CUPS | 600 ML

1 gallon | 3.8 L whole milk

⅓ cup | 80 ml freshly
squeezed lemon juice,
plus more if needed

Scant ¾ teaspoon fine-
grain sea salt

Line a large strainer with a few layers of cheesecloth and set aside until you're ready to use it.

In the meantime, gently bring the milk to a simmer in a large, preferably thick-bottomed pot, over medium heat. Stir often to be sure the milk doesn't scorch at the bottom of the pot. As the milk begins to come to a boil, remove the pot from the heat and add the lemon juice. Stir gently, and curds will start to collect and separate; if you don't see curds forming, add a bit more lemon juice. When a thick layer of curds has formed, use a slotted spoon to transfer the curds to your strainer, gently stir in the salt, and either enjoy it immediately or continue to let it strain for half an hour or so. After straining, you can press the paneer into a mold or shape it and place it on a rimmed plate beneath a heavy pot in the refrigerator, to form a sliceable block of paneer; this will take a few hours. You can reserve some of the whey to use in your next batch of paneer, in place of the lemon juice.

NOTES: Some Indian cooks rinse their curds to rid them of the taste of lemon juice (in some cases, vinegar is used to form the cheese), but I like the hint of lemony brightness, and never bother to rinse.

For a creamier paneer, add 2 cups | 480 ml of cream and increase the amount of lemon juice to ½ cup | 120 ml.

Makhaniya Lassi

crème fraîche ∗ honey ∗ yogurt

*In Jodhpur, locals know
the makhaniya lassi
at the clock tower Mishrilal
Hotel are arguably the best
in Rajasthan. Families,
couples, and workers
mob the establishment,
sitting at orange laminate-
topped tables for a
momentary respite from
the heat and intensity of the
surrounding market area.
The lassi are rich, and thick
enough that a spoon stands
straight up in them. They're
served dolloped with
overwhipped cream.*

*If you can buy cream top
milk and yogurt for this
recipe, it's ideal, but it's not
necessary. You can also
strain the yogurt before
proceeding with the recipe to
increase the thickness.
Make sure that all
ingredients are well chilled
before getting started.*

SERVES 2 TO 4

¼ cup | 60 ml crème fraîche

¼ cup | 60 ml heavy cream

¼ cup | 60 ml water

3 tablespoons runny honey

2 cups | 480 ml plain
full-fat yogurt

Saffron threads, for
garnish (optional)

Combine the crème fraîche and cream in a mixing bowl.
Whisk together until past the point of stiff peaks—you
want the result to look overwhipped cream, a bit clotted
and curdled seeming. Set aside in the refrigerator.

In a glass jar large enough to fit all the ingredients,
whisk the water into the honey until it dissolves. Add the
yogurt, screw on the jar's lid, and give a gentle shake to
combine—aim for a gentle technique, just a few up and
down motions, rather than the vigorous shakes you might
use for a cocktail.

To serve, pour the lassi into well-chilled glasses, dollop
a spoonful of whipped cream along the inside rim of each
glass, and finish with a few strands of saffron.

Variations:

ROSEWATER LASSI: Add 1 teaspoon rosewater, or to taste, to
the jar.

ORANGE BLOSSOM LASSI: Add ½ teaspoon orange blossom
water, or to taste, to the jar.

SAFFRON LASSI: Gently warm the cream (don't let it get too
hot to touch), add a few crushed strands of saffron, allow
to steep for 10 minutes or so, then chill completely before
whipping.

Paratha

wheat flour ∗ clarified butter

I've encountered many flatbreads in my travels, but the flaky, buttery, layered paratha *remains a favorite. It is unleavened, typically inexpensive, and found in many guises. You'll see it plain or stuffed with cheese, potato, cauliflower, or even fenugreek. It might also be served on its own or alongside a range of chutneys or yogurt. And it is incredibly satisfying to make your own at home.*

MAKES 8 PARATHA

1¼ cups | 5.75 oz | 165 grams white whole wheat flour, plus more for dusting

1 cup | 4.5 oz | 115 g all-purpose white flour

1 teaspoon fine-grain sea salt

⅔ cup | 5.3 oz | 150 g melted clarified butter (see page 315), ghee (page 314), or unsalted butter

¾ cup | 180 ml lukewarm water, or more if needed

Combine the flours and salt in a large bowl. Slowly drizzle 2 tablespoons of the melted butter across the flour mixture and use your fingers to work it in. Add most, but not all, of the water and stir by hand or with an electric mixer until it becomes a medium-stiff dough. Add more water a bit at a time, if needed. Continue to knead until the dough becomes silky, smooth, and stretchy—typically 8 to 10 minutes with the hook attachment of a mixer. Shape the dough into a ball, rub with a bit of the melted butter, and set aside, covered, for at least 30 minutes. Divide the dough into 8 pieces and either get ready to shape some *paratha*, or reserve the dough balls on a tightly covered plate in the refrigerator for a day or two. (Bring them back to room temperature before shaping.)

Flatten each ball into a disk on a floured countertop. Using a rolling pin, roll each ball of dough out evenly into a circle 6 or 7 inches | 15 to 18 cm in diameter. Brush with a bit of melted butter and fold into a half circle. Brush the half circle with more butter and fold into a quarter circle. Dust lightly with more flour and roll the triangle out into a flat shape roughly 6 inches | 15 cm in length per side. Throughout the process, dust with flour often enough to keep things from sticking. Complete with the remaining balls and keep the *paratha* in a single layer under a slightly damp cloth.

(continued)

When you're ready to cook the *paratha*, heat a skillet over medium heat. Once hot, add a small amount of butter and place a *paratha* in the pan. Cook until the bottom is deeply brown in spots, 3 to 4 minutes. Rub the top of the *paratha* with a bit more butter and add a tiny sprinkling of salt before flipping. Cook the other side until golden brown, another 3 to 4 minutes, then transfer each *paratha* to a plate or basket lined with a clean cloth. Fold the cloth over the *paratha* to keep them warm as you cook the rest.

Gin & Tonics

Broadly speaking, if you're ordering a drink in India, wine isn't going to be your best option. Beer is a solid choice; my other go-to is gin and tonic. Malaria has historically been a problem in India, and in the 1700s it was discovered that quinine could ward off and treat the disease. I've been told that officers in the British East India Company started adding sugar, water, lime, and part of their ration of gin to the bitter quinine to make it more palatable. Refreshing, bright, and with a history in India, gin and tonics can be a solid drink choice. While I love the classic gin and tonic, I will sometimes infuse the gin with spices I have out for the rest of the meal preparation. This and the following recipe are two standouts.

Saffron Gin & Tonic

lemon * vanilla

MAKES 1 CUP | 240 ML
INFUSED GIN, ENOUGH FOR
8 DRINKS

1 cup | 240 ml gin

Pinch of saffon threads
(about 20)

1 (½-inch | 1.2cm) segment
vanilla bean

Tonic water

Soda water

Lemon

Place the gin in a clean jar. Use a mortar and pestle to crush the saffron threads into a powder. Place 1 tablespoon of the gin into the mortar, rinse the pestle with it, and pour this mixture into the jar of gin. Use a knife to slice the vanilla bean segment lengthwise, then scrape the bean paste from the pod and add it to the gin mixture.

Stir to distribute and break up the vanilla bean paste and allow to sit for 15 minutes. Strain and return the strained gin to the jar; keep it refrigerated until you're ready to mix drinks.

For each drink combine 1 oz | 30 ml infused gin, 1 oz | 30 ml tonic water, and a splash of soda water in a cup with ice cubes and a couple of skinny lemon wedges.

(continued)

Verde Gin & Tonic

coriander * fennel * dill

MAKES 1 CUP | 240 ML
INFUSED GIN, ENOUGH FOR
8 DRINKS

1 teaspoon dried
    coriander seeds

1 teaspoon fennel seeds

1 tablespoon torn fresh dill

Tonic water

Soda water

Orange

Fresh dill sprigs

Place the gin in a clean jar. Use a mortar and pestle to lightly grind the coriander and fennel seeds. Transfer the seeds to the jar of gin and stir in the dill. Allow the mixture to sit for 20 minutes. Strain and return the strained gin to the jar; keep it refrigerated until you're ready to mix drinks.

For each drink combine 1 oz | 30 ml infused gin, 1 oz | 30 ml tonic water, and a splash of soda water in a cup with ice cubes and a couple of skinny orange wedges and tiny sprigs of fresh dill.

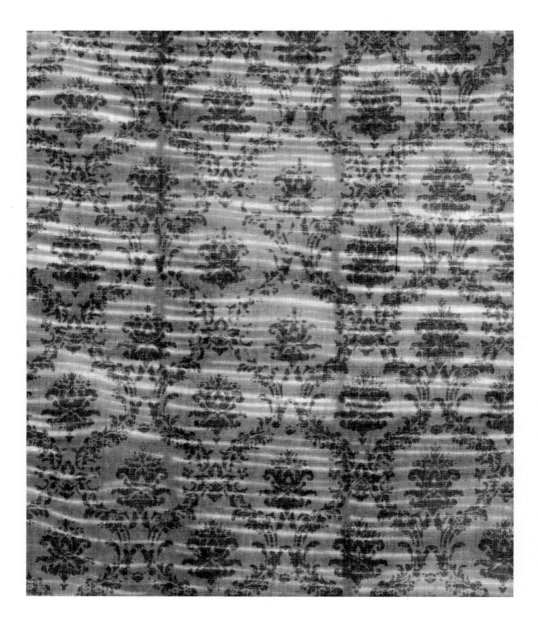

ACCOMPANIMENTS

A Simple Pot of Beans

dried heirloom beans ∗ aromatic vegetables

My technique for cooking beans has evolved a bit over the years. I tend to let them soak for a couple of nights, set out on the counter, sometimes with a splash of whey (see page 321) if I have it on hand. I'll rinse them after a day or so and then cover them with fresh water. The soaking speeds cooking time and imparts a beautiful fullness to each bean that you don't always get when you skip the soaking step.

**MAKES ABOUT
5 CUPS | 25 OZ | 710 G
COOKED BEANS**

1 pound | 455 g dried beans

1 cup | 5 oz | 140 g coarsely chopped aromatic vegetables, such as onions, carrots, celery, and/or dried chiles (optional)

Fine-grain sea salt

Start by picking through the beans carefully, looking for small pebbles or clumps of dirt. Then rinse thoroughly. If you have time to soak the beans, do so—either a day or two ahead, overnight, or starting early in the morning of the day you want to cook them. To do so, place the beans in a large, heavy pot and add enough water to cover by a few inches. Leave at least 4 hours, or as long as a couple of days, refreshing the water after a day.

After soaking, drain the beans and discard the soaking water, then add fresh water in an amount roughly double or triple the volume of beans. If you like, add the vegetables. Bring the pot to a simmer and cook until the beans are tender. Depending on the type of bean and its freshness, cooking time can range from 35 minutes to well over an hour. Sample the beans regularly to gauge doneness.

Season with salt in the last 10 to 15 minutes of cooking time, when the beans are nearly ready. This gives the beans enough time to start absorbing some of the salt but won't cause them to seize up and resist absorption of water, which can result in tough beans. (This is why it's not a good idea to add salt earlier in the cooking process, or use a particularly salty stock.) Drain and freeze any leftover beans; you can add them straight from the freezer to a soup or stew.

Brown Rice

brown rice ✳ sea salt ✳ water

Brown rice is great to have on hand. Make a pot over the weekend, then use it in stir-fries and stews throughout the week. It freezes reasonably well, so keep that in mind if you have rice that might not get used in the coming day or two.

SERVES 4

1½ cups | 10 oz | 285 g short-grain brown rice

2½ cups | 600 ml dashi (page 311) or water

½ teaspoon fine-grain sea salt

Wash and drain the rice a few times in cold water, until the water runs clear. Drain well and set aside for 20 minutes before placing in a saucepan along with the dashi and salt. Cover and bring to a boil over medium-high heat, then reduce to an active simmer. Simmer until the rice is cooked through, 40 to 50 minutes, remove from the heat and allow to sit, still covered, for another 10 minutes before uncovering and fluffing with a fork.

Favorite add-ins:

Stir in 2 tablespoons toasted sesame seeds plus ⅓ cup | 0.25 oz | 8 g chopped garlic chives before serving (pictured).

Stir in 3 tablespoons nori butter (see page 172), or to taste, before serving.

Add 2 tablespoons raw millet to the rice prior to cooking.

For seasoned rice, add 1 tablespoon shoyu, 1 tablespoon mirin, and 2 tablespoons sake to the cooking liquid.

Cultured Honey Butter

cultured buttermilk * heavy cream * raw honey

Home-churned butter is special. Home-churned cultured butter is even better. The depth of flavor and subtle tang from the buttermilk results in the sort of butter you only dream of spreading on good bread, biscuits, or even vegetables. Introduce a good honey to the mix and you have an entirely new realm to explore.

MAKES 1 CUP | 370 G BUTTER

2 tablespoons cultured buttermilk

2 cups | 480 ml heavy cream (the best you can source)

½ cup | 120 ml honey

Flaked sea salt

In a bowl, combine the buttermilk and the cream. Leave out on a countertop (not in direct sunlight) for 12 to 24 hours.

Then, if you have the time, chill the thickened cream. Use an electric mixer with a whisk attachment to beat the cream well past the whipped cream stage, until the liquid completely separates from the solids, about 10 minutes. The butter should come together in a ball.

Press as much of the buttermilk out of the butter as possible and reserve it for another use. Rinse the butter with ice water, pressing it, until the water runs clear of buttermilk. Fold the honey into the butter, along with a sprinkling of salt. Store in an airtight container in the refrigerator for up to 1 week.

NOTE: I typically combine the honey and butter just before serving, so if you don't want to sweeten all of the butter, just fold one part honey into two parts fresh cultured butter.

Dashi

kombu ✳ water

It's hard to explore Japanese cooking without trying to get a handle on the role dashi plays. It's everywhere, running through traditional Japanese cooking the way blood runs through the body. At its most basic, it is a foundation broth—a harmonizing base element—and like Western stocks and broths it comes in many guises. Dashi is very often made from a combination of seaweed and bonito (dried fish flakes). But there is also a wonderful tradition of vegetarian dashi within Buddhist vegetarian temple cuisine (shojin-ryori), *and that is where this version takes its cue. It's the version I tend to keep on hand—light, simple, and straightforward, it's the sort of dashi that provides a whisper of the sea, and a bit of body, but generally allows other ingredients to really shine.*

MAKES 8 CUPS | 2 L

½ oz | 15 g kombu seaweed   8 cups | 2 L water

To start, look over your kombu. If it appears dirty or gritty, wipe it down with a damp cloth. Place the kombu in a pot with the water and allow to sit for at least 1 hour, preferably 2. Alternately, you can place it in the refrigerator overnight.

When you're ready to make the dashi, bring the water and kombu to a simmer over medium heat. Keep it gently simmering for 5 minutes before removing it from the heat. Allow it to sit for another 5 minutes before straining the kombu from the dashi, reserving it for another use if you like (you could use it for a second round of dashi, for example). The dashi is ready to use at this point, and though you should avoid freezing it, it will hold refrigerated for a few days.

Flower Pepper

rose * calendula * peony

I pull petals from whatever edible flowers I have around the house, dry them, and put them to use in simple flower pepper. You can grind the petals and peppercorns in a grinder for a fine grind, or with a mortar and pestle for a coarser one. The latter crushes the peppercorns but leaves the flower petals more intact. There aren't many hard and fast rules here, but I lean toward rose, calendula, hibiscus, peony, jasmine, pansy, and violet for use with sweet-leaning preparations, and keep another grinder with herb blossoms—chives, thyme, basil—and pepper for savory. Lavender can be a nice addition in extreme moderation.

MAKES ¼ CUP | 15 G

1 tablespoon whole black peppercorns

3 tablespoons dried flower petals (rose, calendula, and so on; see Note)

The most convenient way to keep flower pepper on hand is to combine the peppercorns and petals in a dedicated pepper grinder. You can use a single type of petal or a blend. Grind as you need it. As I mention in the headnote, you can also grind using a mortar and pestle.

NOTE: To dry flower petals, arrange in a single layer on a parchment-lined baking sheet and set aside for a week or two, until completely dry. Toss with your fingertips every other day. If you attempt to oven-dry, even at low temperature, you run the risk of losing all the vibrant color in the petals. Dried petals will keep in an airtight container for months.

Ghee

unsalted butter

Ghee is an unsalted butter that has had the milk solids removed after separating them from the butterfat, resulting in beautiful, golden, pure fat with an unusually high smoking point. This means ghee (and its cousin, clarified butter, see Variation) is remarkably stable, even at higher temperatures. Some say the best ghee comes from homemade butter—meaning, you first make butter from fresh cream, and then you turn that butter into delicious ghee. The extra step certainly turns a relatively easy endeavor into something more ambitious, but I thought I'd mention it for those of you who are up for a more extensive process.

Ghee is an ingredient that has been deeply revered in India for many centuries; it's often made from cow's milk (cows are sacred animals in Hinduism), but it is also made from buffalo and sheep's milk. Ayurvedic physicians consider ghee vital for health and well-being— it's recommended for expectant mothers—and it is used to balance and support the body from the inside and the outside—eyes, memory, strength. It's a fat that helps fat-soluble nutrients become available to the body.

Source the best butter you can here, preferably organic. Experiment with cultured and uncultured butters. Also— save any milk foam and milk solids; they're delicious, particularly tossed with brown rice. Either use the solids immediately or refrigerate for up to 3 days.

MAKES ABOUT
1½ CUPS | 360 ML

1 pound | 455 g of the best
    quality unsalted butter
    you can source

Gently melt the butter in a saucepan over medium-low heat. After melting, the butter will separate into three layers. Foam will appear on the top layer, the milk solids will migrate to the bottom of the pan, and clarified butter will float between the two. Let the butter come to a simmer and hold it here until the middle layer becomes fragrant, more golden than when you started, and clear—push any foam on top out of the way to have a peek. The milk solids at the bottom will begin to brown.

At this point it is a matter of preference, you can let the solids lightly brown, or let things progress a bit more. When the ghee is finished, use a spoon or strainer to skim absolutely any remaining foam into a bowl, turn off the heat, and allow things to settle for a minute or so. Carefully pour the golden central layer through a strainer into a clean glass jar, leaving the milk solids at the bottom of the pan. Transfer the solids to the bowl with any foam you've skimmed for another use.

If you are able to remove all the solids from the butter, and you use clean and dry utensils in the jar, the ghee will keep at room temperature for weeks. It can be used as a cooking oil or finishing element.

Variation: **CLARIFIED BUTTER**

The process for making clarified butter is similar to that of making ghee—ghee is simply cooked longer and has more contact with the browning milk solids, lending it a different flavor profile. To make clarified butter, follow the directions for ghee, but don't allow the milk solids to brown.

Ginger Juice

fresh ginger

Fresh ginger juice is one of my go-to ingredients. It adds life and vigor to teas, broths, juices, and dressings. I typically grate peeled knobs of organic, domestic ginger and press it through a sieve or strainer. It takes a bit of time, but nothing brings comparable flavor. If you press a good amount, it freezes nicely in small ice cube trays or in baggies.

MAKES 2 TO 3 TABLESPOONS

A large knob of fresh
  ginger

Grate the ginger (a fine Microplane grater works well) and scoop the grated ginger pulp into a fine-mesh strainer. Use your fingers to press the juice into a bowl. You might find it helpful to make a loose fist and run your knuckles around the sides and bottom of the strainer. (You can, of course, speed the process by using a juicer.)

Hazelnut Spice

poppy seeds * orange zest * espresso * cinnamon

This blend is a warming alternative to dukkah; it's good sprinkled over yogurt and as a finishing element over roasted winter squash or mushrooms. Toasted pecans are great in place of hazelnuts, if those are easier to come by.

MAKES ½ CUP | 2 OZ | 55 G

Dried zest of ½ orange

¼ teaspoon fine-grain sea salt

¼ cup | 1 oz | 30 g toasted hazelnuts

1 tablespoon brown or muscovado sugar

¾ teaspoon ground cinnamon

1 teaspoon finely ground espresso beans (optional)

1 teaspoon poppy seeds (optional)

Use a mortar and pestle to crush the orange zest with the salt. Add the hazelnuts, brown sugar, cinnamon, and espresso and continue to crush until you've achieved a sandy, pebbly consistency. Stir in the poppy seeds. Store in an airtight container in a dark place and use within a few weeks.

Orange Thyme Za'atar

dried orange thyme ✳ sumac ✳ sesame seeds

This is a wonderfully tangy Middle Eastern spice blend I make regularly at home. My secret is this—play around with different varietals of thyme. Lemon thyme, for example, is readily available (and easy to grow). There is a farmer near me growing lavender thyme, and another who grows lime thyme, as well as my favorite for this mixture, orange thyme. Each brings a unique scent, flavor, and personality to the blend.

I find za'atar a welcome counterpoint to the sweetness of deeply roasted delicata squash; swirled generously into yogurt or crème fraîche, it's a brilliant wild card element in big hearty soups; and it's ideal smashed into ripe avocado with a drizzle of great olive oil.

MAKES ⅓ CUP | 9 G

¼ cup | 0.25 oz | 7 g fresh orange thyme leaves, stripped from stems (see Note)

2 teaspoons sumac

Scant ½ teaspoon fine-grain sea salt

1 tablespoon toasted sesame seeds

Preheat the oven to 275°F | 135°C. Place the thyme leaves on a baking sheet and bake until dry, 10 minutes or so—just long enough that they'll crumble between pinched fingers. Let cool. Alternatively, and preferably, arrange fresh thyme sprigs on a paper-lined baking sheet and leave to dry for a week or so.

Use a mortar and pestle to grind the thyme leaves well. If your thyme is at all stemmy or fibrous, sift to remove any larger particles. Transfer to a small bowl and set aside.

Crush the sumac finely with the mortar and pestle, then add the salt and crush with the sumac. Add the reserved thyme and grind all together. Stir in the sesame seeds, taste, and adjust to your liking, perhaps with a bit more salt, or sumac, or sesame seeds. Any za'atar you might not use within 2 to 3 days keeps best refrigerated (or in the freezer); at the very least store it in an airtight container.

Variation: Grind together ¼ cup | 0.25 oz | 7 g lavender thyme leaves, 2 teaspoons sumac, ½ teaspoon fine-grain sea salt, 1 tablespoon black sesame seeds, and 1 teaspoon of crushed dried rose petals.

NOTE: While you can use prepackaged dried thyme here, I prefer to dry my own fresh thyme. The thyme retains a nice green color, the flavor is bright and fresh, and there is none of the mustiness you sometimes get with herbs or spices that are past their prime.

Oregano Drizzle

garlic * parsley * sea salt

I use this on all sorts of things: as a simple dressing for salad greens, over frittatas, tossed with potatoes. It's one of those flavor-packed additions that can make even the simplest preparations special.

MAKES ABOUT
1½ CUPS | 360 ML

1¼ cups | 300 ml extra-virgin olive oil

½ cup | 0.25 oz | 15 g chopped fresh oregano

½ cup | 0.25 oz | 15 g chopped parsley

2 large cloves garlic

Scant ½ teaspoon fine-grain sea salt

Combine ½ cup of the olive oil with the remaining ingredients in a food processor or blender and pulse until well combined. Add the remaining olive oil a bit at a time, pulsing to combine. Taste and add more salt if needed. Store covered in the refrigerator for up to 3 days.

Poached Egg for One

good-quality * free-range egg

Adding a poached egg to soup or salad, or even a slab of good bread, can turn it into a substantial meal. It might take a bit of practice at first, but once you've mastered the poaching technique, you'll find yourself using it often. When I want to make more than one poached egg, I use a two-pan approach (see Variation). This allows me to work through eggs rather quickly and still achieve a nice shape to each egg.

If you aren't eating the eggs immediately, you can keep poached eggs in an ice water bath in the refrigerator for a day or two. Rewarm them, if desired, for about 30 seconds in simmering water before serving.

SERVES 1

2 tablespoons white wine vinegar

1 egg

Fill a saucepan, the deeper the better, with 6 cups | 1.5 L of water. Bring to a gentle simmer. In the meantime, gently crack the egg into a ramekin, then carefully slip it into a fine-mesh strainer over your sink or compost—some of the white will run through and strain off (though if the mesh is too fine, you won't get the desired effect). This minimizes the flyaway whites you normally get. Now carefully slide the egg back into the ramekin.

Stir the vinegar into the simmering water. With a spoon, gently stir the water in the pot to create a vortex. Let the vortex slow a bit—it should be a mellow whirlpool, not anything violent. Slide the egg into the center of the vortex. Let it simmer there for a few minutes, past the point when the white has become opaque. After about 3 minutes carefully lift the egg from the pan with a slotted spoon and poke at it gently with your finger: you can best get a sense of the doneness of the yolk this way. If you like a firmer yolk (like I do), return the egg to the pan for a few more minutes. Remove the egg with a strainer or slotted spoon and use or store.

Variation: To make more than one poached egg, prepare a second pot of simmering water, but don't add the vinegar. Follow the instructions above, and at the point where an egg can hold its shape and be safely moved, carefully transfer it to the second pot of simmering water to finish poaching. Repeat with as many eggs as you need. Alternately, you can simmer water in a large skillet and carefully drop up to 4 eggs, one at a time, into the skillet. They won't be as pretty, but the process is certainly faster and simpler, and I tend to use this technique most often.

Whey & Labneh

plain yogurt * sea salt

With all its beneficial probiotic properties, I like to keep whey on hand to use in everything from baked goods to soups, dressings, and drinks. You can use it to easily culture grains and legumes you're soaking, which helps make the nutrients in them more bioavailable. Whey keeps in the refrigerator for a week or two; extra whey is also happy to be frozen.

One way to start your supply of whey is to make labneh or strained yogurt. The liquid that comes off the yogurt is the whey, and the labneh can be used in many ways—as a spread; rolled into balls, rolled in za'atar (see page 318), and drizzled with olive oil; or combined with an endless spectrum of fruit purees or spices to give it whatever character you like.

This recipe uses a large container (1 quart | 32 oz | 910 g) of yogurt, which strains down quite a lot. That said, if you think you'll have a hard time using this much labneh, halve the recipe. The longer you let the yogurt strain, the thicker it gets.

MAKES ABOUT
2 CUPS | 16 OZ | 455 G
OF LABNEH AND
2 CUPS | 480 ML OF WHEY

¼ teaspoon fine-grain
sea salt

1 quart | 32 oz | 910 g plain
full-fat yogurt

Arrange a fine-mesh strainer over a deep bowl. Stir the salt into the yogurt, then pour the yogurt into the strainer to drain. If you don't have a strainer, simply line a deep bowl with a double layer of cheesecloth. Stir the salt into the yogurt and pour it into the cheesecloth. Bring the cloth together into a bundle and secure with a string. Hang the bundle over a bowl (or wide pitcher), making sure the bottom of the cheesecloth is suspended in air (you don't want it sitting in the liquid). One option is to secure the bundle to a wooden spoon.

(continued)

Cover the whole contraption and refrigerate for at least 24 hours, but go longer if you like—it's all about personal preference. Much of the liquid will drain out and the yogurt will thicken. Remove the labneh from the strainer or cloth and the whey from the bowl and use or store both.

ACKNOWLEDGMENTS

I loved working on this book in part because of its subject and scope, but also because of the generous people who contributed to the process. I'm thankful and indebted to many.

Wayne, there's no one I'd rather see the world with. Let's book a flight.

Aaron Wehner, Julie Bennett, Michele Crim, Serena Sigona, Hannah Rahill, Kristin Casemore, Daniel Wikey, Chloe Xenia Rawlins, and everyone at Ten Speed Press, your support and insight is always appreciated. Thank you for consistently hearing me out, for being open to exploring new ideas, and for continually making me feel like part of the family. Aaron, thank you for your enthusiasm for this one from go, and Julie, for gracefully guiding it through the process. Toni Tajima, I won the design lottery back when we did *Super Natural Cooking*, and I'm thankful we've been together since.

Tina Dang and Emelie Griffin, my kitchen angels; I'm already missing our lunches together.

Heather, Mark, and Jack Ruder and Gary and Janelle Swanson, my family.

There are a whole host of individuals who, in one way or another, helped, inspired, or contributed to the making of this book: Nikki Graham, Oliver Fross and Naya Peterson, Colleen Hennessey, Nikole Herriott, Sarah Lonsdale, Steve Sando, Eric Gower, Dorie Greenspan, Lanha Hong-Porretta, Paula Wolfert, Leah Rosenberg, Ashrf and Shelly Amasri, Malinda Reich, Carol Hacker, Grace Young, Melissa Millward, Rachel Bracken Singh and Pritam Singh, Owen Seitel, Clotilde Dusoulier and Maxence Bernard, Shankar Singh, Elizabeth David, Dulcie May Booker, Curtis Cate, Anna Jones, Deborah Madison, Samin Nosrat, Elissa Altman, Jen Altman, Amanda Gilligan, Susannah Conway, and Maryam Montague. My Saturday morning market coffee clan: Bonni Evensen, Chanda Williams, and Jamie Litchmann.

INDEX

All photographs are by Heidi Swanson with the exception of those noted here:
pages 57, 74–5, 103, 112–13, 136, 166, 224 (bottom), 291 and 296–7 by Wayne Bremser.

Library of Congress Cataloging-in-Publication Data
Swanson, Heidi, 1973–
Near & far : recipes inspired by home and travels / Heidi Swanson. —
First edition.
    pages cm
Includes bibliographical references and index.
1. International cooking. I. Title. II. Title: Near and far.
TX725.A1S89 2015
641.59—dc23

                2014047586

Hardcover ISBN: 978-1-60774-549-5
eBook ISBN: 978-1-60774-550-1

Printed in China

Design by Toni Tajima

10 9 8 7 6 5 4 3 2 1

First Edition